Praise for
A Big-Enough God

"Should prove of particular interest to lovers of language who delight in spiritual dimensions of mathematical speculation and scientific discovery as well as formal theology. That the book took shape in a Lenten series of lectures to a group of Anglican clergy seems to have heightened Maitland's awareness of the role of amateur as lover, and she shares this to good effect with readers. As she notes, she is flirting with ideas, inviting readers to do the same."

—*Booklist*

"Provides both food for thought and a more user-friendly deity for disaffected Christians."

—*Kirkus Reviews*

D1113251

ALSO BY SARA MAITLAND

FICTION

Ancestral Truths

Three Times Table

Virgin Territory

A Book of Spells

Telling Tales

Daughter of Jerusalem

NONFICTION

A Map of the New Country:
Women and Christianity

The Rushdie File
(editor, with Lisa Appignanesi)

BIOGRAPHY

Vesta Tilley

A BIG-ENOUGH GOD

A FEMINIST'S SEARCH FOR A JOYFUL THEOLOGY

Sara Maitland

RIVERHEAD BOOKS, NEW YORK

Riverhead Books
Published by The Berkley Publishing Group
200 Madison Avenue
New York, New York 10016

Extracts from Annie Dillard, *Pilgrim at Tinker Creek*, on pp. 40–41, 42, and 64 are reproduced by permission of HarperCollins, USA, and Random House, UK; from *A Dream of the Rood*, translated by Charles Kennedy, on p. 132 by permission of Oxford University Press, Inc., New York; from Anne Sexton, "The Rowing Endeth" in *The Awful Rowing Toward God* (copyright © 1975 by Loring Conant Jr, Executor of the Estate of Anne Sexton, all rights reserved), on pp. 137–38 by permission of Houghton Mifflin Co. and Sterling Lord Literistic; and the poem by Michelene Wandor on pp. 138–39 by permission of Pluto Press.

Copyright © 1995 by Sara Maitland
Cover design by Dale Fiorillo
Cover art: *Porta Norde, annunciazione* by Ghiberti, Firenze Battistero.
Courtesy of Scala/Art Resource, N.Y.

Reprinted by arrangement with Henry Holt and Company, Inc.
Originally published in Great Britain in 1995 by Mowbray, an imprint of Cassell PLC.
First published in the United States in 1995 by Henry Holt and Company, Inc.
Henry Holt and Company, Inc. ISBN: 0-8050-4183-4
First Riverhead trade paperback edition: December 1996

The Putnam Berkley World Wide Web site address is
http://www.berkley.com/berkley

The Library of Congress Cataloging-in-Publication Data
Maitland, Sara.
   A big-enough God : a feminist's search for a joyful theology /
Sara Maitland. — 1st Riverhead ed.
     p.   cm
   Originally published : New York : H. Holt, 1995.
   Includes bibliographical references.
   ISBN 1-57322-574-6
   1. Creation. 2. Theology—Forecasting. 3. Feminist theology.
I. Title.
   695.M35 1996   96-7890
   1.7'65—dc20   CIP

Printed in the United States of America

10 9 8 7 6 5 4 3 2 1

For

RICHARD COLES

with love and thanks

I would also like to thank Ros Hunt, Janet Batsleer, Jenny Barrett, Alan Green, Sabine Butzlaf, Ken Leech, Trevor Richardson, James Hanvey, Rowan Williams, Alan Mould, Michael Shier, and Arther Peacocke for their assorted assistance; Arthur Partridge of Corpus Christi, Cambridge, for curbing my exuberance and correcting my science; Judith Longman of Mowbray; and Fr Alan Scott and the people of St Mary's Stoke Newington, with whom I first explored many of the ideas in the book.

Much of the material in this book was worked out in a series of four lectures given in Lent 1992, to the Anglican clergy of the Stepney Episcopal Area of the Diocese of London. Thanks are due to Jim Thompson, then Bishop of Stepney, and to his Archdeacon; and to everyone who attended the lectures.

Contents

Introduction   1

1   *Dice throwing made easy*   25

2   *What am I?*   68

3   *Artful theology*   108

4   *Angelic woodlice and other delights*   149

A BIG-
ENOUGH
GOD

Introduction

It is a crafty, though not altogether honest, ploy to apologize for a book right at the beginning: it disarms the critic and protects the writer in one cheap move. It is also, interestingly, a device frequently used by women when they are about to exercise power.

'I know I have the body of a weak and feeble woman', begins Queen Elizabeth I, before asserting her sovereign power, and socking it to her navy at Greenwich in what must be one of the best gung-ho militaristic polemics in the English language . . . 'but I have the heart and stomach of a King', she goes on, 'and of a King of England too.'[1]

> I shall have to make use of some comparisons, for which I would like to apologize, since I am a woman I write simply what I am ordered to write. But this spiritual language is so difficult to use for anyone like myself who has not gone through studies that . . . it may be that most of the time I won't get it right. Seeing so much stupidity will provide some amusement for you.[2]

writes Teresa of Avila, just to cover herself as she begins yet another savage attack on the Spanish hierarchy, and the spiritual conventions of her time.

Instinctively I wanted to begin this book with a quotation from Psalm 131.

> Lord, I am not high-minded: I have no proud looks;
> I do not exercise myself in great matters which are too
> high for me.

> Truly I have set my soul in silence and peace; as a
> weaned child on its mother's breast so even is my
> soul.

Unlike St Teresa and Elizabeth Tudor and countless other women who used this technique, or write under male *noms de plume* or found other, similar, cover-ups for their own temerity for real and material reasons of oppression, I am a daughter of feminism; I know for a certainty that my impulse to apologize is internal. My argument, in this book, is that those of us who are Christians in these pregnant years leading up to the twenty-first century have nothing to be afraid or ashamed of—and so it is interestingly something about inferiority and self-subjection that leads me to go to even the lengths of apologizing for not apologizing.

I do not believe that the matters I am going to discuss here are 'too high for me' as the psalmist puts it. They are not too high for anyone. It is abundantly clear that if God exists she exists as a God who wishes to reveal herself; who labours constantly and complexly in her relationships with the creation, both individual and communal, tossing down clues and invitations and introductory notes here, there and everywhere like an ambitious hostess: a God who yearns to be loved and known and engaged with. Nothing else explains the business of creating *anything at all*. If the process of knowing and believing feels complex and difficult this must surely be because what is being revealed is a depth of complexity, of intricacy and enormity that ought to delight us but usually scares us. The desire to reduce it all to a tidy little formula is irresistible and must be resisted: in the last count why bother about a tiny little, simple God who is slightly less complicated than the workings of my own mind?

This year, after three centuries of effort, mathematicians

have (probably) found a proof of Fermat's Last Theorem. This is a very simple little theorem on paper: that for the proposition

$$X^n + Y^n = Z^n$$

there are no solutions for any whole number where n is higher than 2. I am not asking you to get excited about this—although actually it is very exciting—but simply to face the fact that it has taken some of the best abstract thinkers in Western history over 300 years of devoted work to crack this nut. It took nearly three hours to demonstrate something as simple as this one line. (Even now it will take several years for those who can understand how it was done, to check that it was done right.) Why ever *should* we think that 'proving' or explaining the God who is both transcendent and immanent, who holds the universe in a hand which sets it free, who can 'do' both black holes and the pure giggles of a ticklish baby, will be easy? Nonetheless here is a God challenging, prodding, inspiring, moving people to give it a try. We are all invited to come and play this game; and no one is excluded. I draw much comfort, indeed, from the fact that Fermat, the French lawyer after whom this particular equation is known, was an amateur mathematician rather than a professional—and he did not find this matter too high for him.[3]

This book grew out of an invitation to give a series of Lent lectures to the clergy of the Church of England's Stepney Episcopal Area—that is to the Anglican clergy of inner East London (and anyone else who wanted to attend). My official brief for these lectures was to offer these professional Christians 'something that might help them in their spiritual journeys'. This was a pretty tall order. Later on in the book I hope to explore the relationship of what is usually called 'spirituality' to what it is to be a person, and one of the things that I am convinced of is that the process of growth towards

God is also a process of growth towards oneself, and one's own self—because of the sort of God we have—is different from any other self. In this sense I cannot possibly know what will 'help' anyone—and doubt very much if there is anything that will help everyone at once. All I can do really is tell you about some things that have interested or amused me, as part of the engagement to see what it is that God wants to be known—and see what happens.

Because of the necessarily subjective nature of this enterprise, I would like to say something first about myself. Something about how I came to be the sort of person who does the sort of theology I do. This narrative seems important because there are no other criteria against which you can test the usefulness or accuracy of what I am going to say.

I was born in 1950 into a large and prosperous Scottish family, and was brought up as a Presbyterian. In Scotland the Presbyterian Church (The Church of Scotland) is established, in exactly the same way that Episcopalianism (The Church of England, The Anglican Communion) is established in England. In fact, slightly mysteriously, the Queen is the supreme governor, the head, of both churches simultaneously.

Out of that background I brought a great love of the Bible and a generally warm feeling about Christianity and community. I did not however discover there any sense of 'personal conversion', of passion or commitment. As a teenager the mantle of Christianity simply slipped off: there was nothing traumatic or difficult about it, no violent or exciting experience of lapsing—faith simply was not one of the things we thought or felt or talked about.

Retrospectively I think I was remarkably lucky: when in the early seventies I encountered God again it was freely—I carried, I think, little guilt in relation to her; little sense that God was on my family's side and therefore opposed to my adulthood—which by now incorporated socialism, feminism, and libertarianism.

Nowadays there is so much apology and shamefacedness about the 1960s that it is hard to say clearly and nondefensively that I think something happened in those years so profound and exciting and liberating that I can feel only pity for people who were around then and now need to deny the vitality and inspiration of those years. Feminism rose out of that exuberance and, for us western children at least, gave us a living taste of the apostolic virtues of hope, faith and love.

It was this conviction of enormous possibility that brought me back to thinking about God. I have done my time in analysis and am aware how dubious this may sound, but I at least am convinced by my own narrative. It was not that I poked my head over the parapet and was so frightened by what I saw that I scuttled back to the securities of childhood. It was exactly the reverse: made brave by hope and anger, I was tough enough for the enormous God whom I met.

In 1972 I became an Anglican (Episcopalian). In the same year I published my first work of fiction, got married to an American who was later to become an Anglican priest, and got pregnant. It was a good year.

I was deeply happy as an extremist catholic Anglican for many years. It was fun; it was colorful, gossipy, close-knit, extravagant and deeply ironic. We were justified sinners, at odds with the establishment. We knew, I think healthily, that much of our position was preposterous.

'If that's what you think,' a bishop said to a priest friend of mine, 'why on earth don't you become a Roman Catholic?'

'Oh,' he said serenely, 'I could never be a priest in a church where I can't laugh at myself.' (He is a Roman Catholic too now; I hope he is still laughing.)

There was an emergent Christian feminism growing in the UK which for me balanced the ecclesial conservatism of much Anglo-Catholicism; but equally the strongly sacramental constructions of high-church liturgical practice balanced the rationalist and individualist tendencies of much feminist theory.

But in the end I discovered with considerable sorrow that it is nearly impossible for a radical to be comfortable in an established church—for a Republican to accept that the Queen appoints the bishops, and that the bishops sit in the House of Lords and create the statute law. And, in Britain, this is inextricably entangled in the whole issue of class and conservatism which we as a nation have never been able to address. An established and national church, by its nature, cannot be a big-enough church. Liberal rationalism, an almost inevitable consequence of establishment in a multifaith secular society, cannot generate a big-enough theological base. Particularly I would say white, colonialist, male, liberal rationalism, which proceeds from a premise of normativeness; that has a historic trust in its own good sense and reasonableness.

In 1993 I became a Roman Catholic; there has been no doctrinal nor liturgical change for me, merely a repositioning of my relationship to authority; a reaffirmation, despite its many sillinesses (and I must say wrongnesses) that a church can, and must, be universal, can be large scale through time and space—can indeed be big enough.

This is a churchy narrative. There is another narrative that runs alongside it, interwoven with it, but separate. The narrative of the relationship of a self with her God. The self, myself, while wrestling with these issues was also—in my own writing, in my own praying, in my own loving—more and more encountering a strange and enormous God. A God who reflected back to me always a tension between beauty and suffering; between joy and sinfulness; between past and present; between the individual and the community. By community I do not just mean the contemporary society in which I live but a community of history and language and symbol and image. A community of shared signs, of patterned knowledge and patterned failure of knowledge too.

More and more I found that I do not base such frail faith as I have on the feeling of 'what a friend I have in Jesus' but rather on the continual inescapable sense of the power and the mystery and the danger and the profligacy of it all. I mean *all*, from the bizarre goings-on inside each atom, right through to the social complexity of history and class and gender and race and individual experience.

It is the job of credal religion and of art to try and structure that tension intellectually and emotionally, both to contain and to reveal it. Form it is called, form and structure and genre. I cling to orthodoxy in theology and to form in cultural production. The challenge is in the balance; to go as near to the edge, as near to the power and the mystery and the danger as possible without collapsing into chaos. My rampant individualism—especially as feminism and socialism too become more individualistic—needs the counterweight of a rigorous orthodoxy; needs the clear demanding structures to ballast me with connectedness, a protection against the dangerous voyages of the imagination, and to ensure my return to sanity and to home.

I am not a theologian. I am a Christian, a feminist and a writer: a fictionalizer, a liar in Plato's definition. I rather incline to the definition of theology as (1) the art of telling stories about the divine and (2) the art of listening to those stories. I have very little training in formal theology—and even less in formal philosophy.

This is not an apology, it is a statement of fact.

When it comes to theology I am, as Fermat was to mathematics, in the literal sense of the word, an amateur—a lover. As a lover I cannot help but desire that theology should be more playful, more open, more giving, should respond to me more sexily than is its habit: what you are going to get in the next four chapters is an unashamed and blatant attempt at seduction, and you are free therefore to see it as flirting with the issues if you so choose.

In the second place, what I am mainly planning to do is report on my own search for a theology that I can make work, here in a declining Western imperialist capitalist state, and here in the 1990s and in my own personal life (which is a white, professional, middle-aged woman's life). Of course I would like to convince you that I am engaged in an entirely neutral search for Truth, and that my mind is completely open to any and all promptings of the Spirit. However honesty obliges me to admit that this is untrue: I come to the task with distinct prejudices—both the ones I know about and the ones I don't. It feels important to me to come clean at least about the ones I am aware of.

I am not simply looking; I am looking *for* a theology which has a certain prerequisite framework. It has to be a theology that leads to and sustains an anthropology and an ethics which affirm *difference* as something desirable. We are, quite simply, not 'all the same underneath': a person as person is not androgynous, classless, colourless—nor, most importantly perhaps, timeless. Personhood, what it is to be a self, as I shall argue in Chapter 2, is to be created within particularity (within time and space). Difference exists—a stone is not a loaf of bread. Is part of Jesus' objection to turning stones into bread, when hungry in the wilderness, precisely an acknowledgement that stones too have their rights? There seems in all of us to be an enormous resistance to the idea that a thing can simply be different from another thing (usually with *my*self as the normative thing and divergence from that as abnormal) without becoming better or worse. Yet the scandal of particularity,[4] the fact of the Incarnation, holds up difference, specificity, as desirable. Moreover if difference and diversity are not good in themselves then it is a little difficult to see how this can possibly be the best of all possible worlds—this cosmos in which difference proliferates and the number of insect species is uncountable. The theology I am looking for must affirm the reality of difference; call attention to it; honour and proclaim it as part of the glory. For unless difference is proclaimed the possibility of communicating in love with each other, let alone with God who is manifestly and necessarily different from us, is patently impossible.

Next, this theology has to be a theology which is more than merely consolatory; which is effective towards political and social change; which has transformative potential. Because of that, it has to be a theology that links, rather than divides, communities of the oppressed. This means I cannot work towards a theology that requires—or, ideally, even allows—the oppression of other marginalized communities as the price of the liberation of my own community, whatever that is—the community of women, the community of feminist theologians, the community of mothers, of people who live in the East End of London, of a particular class or nationality. And *that* means, among other things, that justice issues can never be detached from metaphysical issues: mysticism and ethics are inextricably bound together; and we have to hold up that knot with pride.

These are two expansionist requirements. However I also have restrictive, or prescriptive, requirements of my theology. The theology I am searching for has to be a theology which affirms that personal salvation and communal renewal are realities; and are wrought through the Incarnation, passion, resurrection and ascension of Jesus Christ, who is both a Jewish carpenter with messianic convictions from Roman Palestine *and* the pre-existent divine Logos, who was 'in the beginning before all worlds'. (This is a requirement for me, because like most progressive theologians I do not want a theology which runs counter to, or does not recognize, the reality and validity of my own lived experience.)

It has also to be a theology grounded in revelation: I believe in Christianity as a *revealed* religion. I shall return to this idea fairly frequently, but for the meantime I would just like to say that by revelation I mean that God in the strictly logical or rational sense is finally unknowable, undemonstrable. God has revealed and continues to reveal God, quite simply, as a gift.

I say 'quite simply' but of course it isn't simple at all. God obviously enjoys crossword puzzles. God's self-revelation seems to be, as it were, in code: a set of cryptic clues. Of course this is partly because God is cleverer than we are; can use more languages, more types of discourse than we can even dream of. God is up to something larger, more complex and more refined than we seem able to imagine. It may also be because of material limitations—just as the physical structure of how it is to be a human being will prevent anyone ever running a 3-second mile, so the physical/neural structure of how it is to be human beings may actually make it impossible for us to frame a language or a thought that embraces eternity. We exist in time, we need time and place to be humans, but that may simply make it impossible for us to perceive, to comprehend in 'not-time'. Nevertheless the unknowability of God is to some extent set aside by God. We cannot claim this as a right, nor prove it, nor own it. What we know of God, we know from God; and a theology that proceeds on any other terms is for me deficient.

Finally, this workable theology has to be, for me—speaking not just personally but passionately—a theology which allows for, and encourages the belief in, what I will call a Big-Enough God—a God who is in the final count larger, cleverer, more infinite than her creation or my theology can describe her. God cannot be limited by her own generosity. That we can know nothing of God which is not given to us as a free gift does not mean that God has to give everything, or cannot be more and other than is revealed. Nonetheless there is some comfort, some feathered wing under which to shelter here; if God is true, is Truth, then God must be coherent, integrated; God can certainly be more and other than is revealed, but cannot be contradictory to her self-revelation, so that what is revealed will not be contradicted by that which is not revealed (assuming here, that we interpret the revelation truthfully—and of that we cannot be certain).

These are the broad terms within which I am trying to proceed with my theological life. What I am hoping to do in this book is look at one particular source of revelation. To look at, and think about, God as 'the maker of heaven and earth', at God as creator.

It is sad that this needs further clarification really, but I am afraid that it does. According to the teaching of Christianity, there are three sources of revelation:

(1) The holy Scriptures—the canonical writings commonly called the Bible (which means that this source of revelation is already mediated by the second source, since it was the post-apostolic Church which fixed the canon, and not without debate);

(2) The tradition—the continual meditation on and interpretation of the Scriptures and the creation within history by the Christian community, more commonly called the Church;

(3) The creation.

Within Anglicanism, the style of Christianity in which I first learned theology, the third source is more often called reason (Scripture, tradition and reason are the three sources of revelation). But it has become clear that there are particular problems with this word. The first difficulty is that it implies that the Scriptures and the tradition are somehow unreasonable. For those people who maintain a finger-of-God, in-errant-dictation understanding of Scripture, reasonableness is not very important; but any more modern hermeneutic requires there to be a certain linguistic and theological reasonableness (coherence) within Scripture itself. In the same way the idea that there can be any authority in a totally illogical, unreasoned, irrational mediation and interpretation—that the tradition is devoid of reason—is fairly senseless.

Even more importantly perhaps, scientism (the view that the

scientific method provides the key to total and absolute Truth in the same way that biblical fundamentalists hold that the Bible does) has stolen the meaning from the word reason. The seventeenth-century Anglican divines who saw reason as a source of revelation did not mean anything like the instrument of calculation, classification and systematization which the word usually signifies now. For them, reason was something intrinsic not external, and far from alienating human beings from the creation sprang up from it in the widest sense. Jeremy Taylor, the seventeenth-century theologian, wrote:

> Reason is such a box of quicksilver that it abides nowhere: it dwells in no settled mansion; it is like a dove's neck, or a changeable taffeta; it looks to me otherwise than it looks to you who do not stand in the same light as I do . . . The heart of reason, that vital and most sensible part, in which it can only be conquered fairly, is like an ambulatory essence and not fixed: it wanders up and down like a floating island, or like that which we call the life blood.[5]

Sensing that there is some problem with the traditional articulation of this third source of revelation as 'reason', people—and particularly feminist theologians[6]—have tried out various alternatives. In particular, some people have argued that there needs to be a recognized fourth source of revelation, sometimes called 'individual conscience' or 'personal experience'. However, the idea of 'individual conscience' falters before our increased understanding of the complexity of ideas like 'individual' and the realization that conscience itself is not a free, independent entity, but is constructed within culture and within history through all the dynamics that psycholinguistics have revealed.

The suggestion that 'personal experience' is an independent source of knowledge of God is much favoured by radical and progressive theologies, and is an idea to which I used to ascribe with some vigour. However I would now like to repent publicly of this error. To suggest that 'experience' has an independent life; that it somehow happens *outside* of the created order, outside time and history and culture, is either to limit God to an initial trigger-action shotgun creation—the old Newtonian clock-maker God of a clockwork universe—or it is to place ourselves, and our experience, outside of creation as though creation was projected onto a screen while we all sat in the audience: a sort of arty television documentary about God, which we, or at least our immortal souls, could observe and learn from in a posture of detachment. This possibility is ruled out by our sinfulness, by the Incarnation, and by the observations of twentieth-century physicists who have demonstrated first that the observer affects the experiment, the thing observed (Einstein's Relativity and Heisenberg's Uncertainty Principle), and more recently still that there is *no* place and *no* time 'outside' the creation in which we *could* sit and 'experience' the show (Hawking's quantum smear at the moment of the Big Bang).

I would now argue that the problem is not that we need a new name for, or a further source of, revelation, but that, on the contrary, we need to accept all the data we have got: we, you and me, our experience, identity, history, personality, our *selves*, are an integral part of the revelation of God in creation. Our bones are the bones of the old red stars; and our cherished egos are constructed and reconstructed daily by history and culture and fashion and, above all and within all, by time. God created, we believe, *ex nihilo* and—as post-Einsteinian physics has stressed—time, like space, is intrinsic to the order of the cosmos. There was no time before the creation; time came into existence with space, they are inextricably connected and there is no escape, no loophole, no separation, no detachment. There is no experience outside the creativity of God.

Mathematicians argue frequently that elegance, or beauty, is part of mathematical proof, so I have no shame in suggesting that the threefold nature of revelation, given the Being of a threefold God, is profoundly satisfactory, is elegant, is beautiful, and therefore is more likely to be true than the dragging in of extra and unnecessary axioms: orthodoxy is very often immensely radical in a rather irritating way.

The other problem in trying to write about revelation in creation is that, after a long period of neglect, usually driven by interested parties—biblical fundamentalists who wished to prioritize Scripture and ecclesiological fundamentalists who wished to claim extortionate authority for tradition—so-called creationist theology has leapt back into fashion by making equally fundamentalist claims for itself. Scripture 'doesn't work' and the 'tradition'—now called 'the *institutional* Church'—is the cause of all our woes, being power-mad and sin-and-guilt obsessed. There is only one true source of knowledge of God, these writers claim, and that is 'nature' or 'Mother Earth' or 'creation', which is somehow uncontaminated and innocent. Oddly enough this line of thought, which claims to be treating the created order with such integrity, falls precisely into the old dualist error of separating humanity from the matter, the hard stuff, the material which is the created order. Human beings and their guilt and their sin and their Scripture and their tradition and their history are integrally, absolutely, part of creation. This nasty messy stuff out of which we are made does not manifest itself only in rainbows and the sweet nurturing of Mother Earth—but equally in volcanoes and greed and famine and power.

When, then, I say that this book is about creation as a source of revelation I do not mean that it is about the most important, the primary or the only real source of revelation. I mean that creation is *one of the sources* of revelation and, as it happens, it is the one that this book is about. This can be taken as a little lesson in what I was trying to say about difference: because I am writing about one thing it should not imply a derogation of other different things. I believe that God desires to be known, as far as we are able to do so. To this end we are offered a variety of sources of divine knowledge. The three recognized by the Christian Church are Scripture, tradition and creation, and it is about this last that I am planning to write.

I will be suggesting however that many Christians in the West (and I dare say elsewhere) have actually lost their way fighting between the first two, and that accepting more seriously the third source of revelation in fact eases the tensions between the first two, as well as throwing new complexities and delights into the treasure-hunt which God apparently wants us to play.

On the one hand you can see these sources as limitations: Christians aren't allowed just to make it up ourselves, nor to try and deduce it by abstract rationality. On the other hand this tripartite division is simply a way of clarifying that almost *everything* falls into one category or the other; and in this sense they are meant to enlarge and liberate our understanding of God, not limit or restrict it. The only 'rules' are that the three sources cannot be contradictory. However, although they can't be contradictory they don't necessarily have to be seamlessly coherent or compatible. Jesus is fully human and fully divine; these are incompatible but complementary (just as in relation to light, Niels Bohr and others have shown that wave-like and particle-like descriptions are incompatible but complementary) and in revelation are not contradictory.

Although many of us have grown up gratefully with St Patrick's clover-leaf image of the Trinity—three leaves making up one clover leaf—there is always room for some new imagery as well. My favourite model of the Trinity is that it is like a child's pigtail. If the Trinity is seen as a plait—three equal strands, smoothly interrelated—there are some advantages. Firstly, you can tear one of the leaves off a clover threesome and leave the other two still related, but if you pull one of the strands out of a plait the whole thing collapses. Inasmuch as there is a trinitarian God, this threefold revelation makes perfect sense, and obviously the same thing applies: you cannot have any two of the sources without the third because the whole thing falls apart. At times, when plaiting, it is important to look at the whole pigtail and check that the hair has been reasonably accurately divided into three. Both the Orthodox Churches of the East and the charismatic movement have suggested that perhaps the mainstream churches of the West have become excessively Christocentric—that their emphasis on the second person of the Trinity has made the pigtail somewhat lopsided. In the same way I would suggest that perhaps we have allowed the strand of revelation in creation to get rather too skinny; that God's rôle as creator and sustainer of the universe needs some fleshing out, some extra weight.

I think this is especially true at the moment because the scientific materialists seem to have frightened a lot of Christians badly. Scared of what we might find, we seem stubbornly to turn our back on the thrilling truths that scientists are offering us. This has been going on since Galileo, but it has got worse recently—first with evolutionary theory and now with post-Einsteinian physics and most immediately with cosmology. I was a bit surprised in 1992, when they discovered the radio-wave fluctuations that are necessary to the Big Bang scenario, that most of the serious newspapers felt it incumbent on them to get in a theologian to say we could still go on believing in God if we wanted to. I was taken aback, really, that anyone should feel that their faith might be shaken by something so stunningly powerful and beautiful as this new creation narrative; by something as impressive as the creative and imaginative energy that had gone into discovering it; and the international solidarity and sharing of labour that had enabled the discovery. The waves themselves, and the human success in detecting them, seemed powerfully reassuring to my conviction in the fertility and power of God.

However, I accept that the fear is there. It does not need to be—we have always to handle the other sources of our faith and we never expected to prove the existence of God by the scientific method (equally, we need not expect scientists to prove the non-existence of God either). There have been a great number of books written in the last few years trying to 'prove' one thing or another about God by examining contemporary science. That is not my project: I believe in God as creator and redeemer. Believing in God as creator, I therefore believe that we can learn something about the nature of the God who created *this* set of things, things which work in *this* particular way. Therefore the more we know about what is there and how it works, the more we can perhaps know about God—'we can know the creator through the creatures', as St Teresa puts it.[7] I do not have the time, the energy or the knowledge to pick through the galaxies or plunge into the atoms—or even into the social sciences—looking for evidence *for* God. I know that God exists, from evidence obtained elsewhere, and am convinced that trying to 'prove God' from our scientific discoveries is as doomed to failure as the medieval attempt to 'prove God' through philosophic methods.

> Does the fish soar to find the ocean.
> The eagle plunge to find the air—
> That we ask of the stars in motion
> If they have rumour of thee there?
> Not where the wheeling systems darken,
> And our benumb'd conceiving soars!—
> The drift of pinions, would we hearken,
> Beats at our own clay-shuttered doors.[8]

What I have in mind instead is a more serious creation theology—that is a creative creation theology; one that contemplates, I hope poetically and imaginatively, all the data that our God's creation gives us, looking, not for evidence *for* God, but for the evidence *of* God: the smudges of the divine finger-prints, the stray clues left *in situ*, the brush marks of a great artist, which must inevitably be there, and which—as part of that creation—God has given us the curiosity, the intelligence and the consciousness to explore. Lots of it, to encourage you, is, unsurprisingly but delightfully, very, very beautiful.

For these reasons, in the chapters that follow, I have tried to understand 'science' in the widest sense. I shall look, how-ever superficially, at a large range of contemporary knowl-edge, new things we have learned; not just about the far-flung dancing universes out beyond the cosmic horizon, but also about human beings, biologically and socially; about ideas and ideology and language; the way people relate to each other and to their own creations and creativities; about cul-ture, and about personhood.

I see the project of this book not being a scientific one, but a meditation, a contemplation of God in this particular as-pect of revelation.

It is fair, however, to warn readers at the outset that al-though I have no problem at all about the existence of God, I do have a problem with much of the language that is used about God; and I am aware that many people will have a problem with the language I use about God. Throughout this book I have used female pronouns when writing about God. So perhaps it is important to say that I believe I am writing about the same God as the Christian tradition has al-ways tried to speak about. Specifically, I do not want to deny either the Trinity in Unity, or the Fatherhood of the first person of the Trinity. In this sense I believe that saying 'Our Father who art in heaven' is a radical critique of patriarchy rather than an affirmation of it. 'Call no man father', we are told in the gospel.

There is a grammatical problem here, a real inflexibility in the way our language works. When I use the word 'she' of God I am trying to say something about the way the Church's tradition is both right and profoundly abusive. I tried to explain how I handled this contradiction in a Lent meditation prepared for radio in 1993. My piece, one in a longer series of meditations on the Apostles' Creed, was based on the opening phrase, 'I believe in God, the Father Almighty'. It may help those people who find female language for God difficult if I quote some of that meditation here:

> Of course she is Father. She is Father Almighty.
>
> She is Father because she is all things, and all things have their being in and from her, including presumably earthly fathers, like earthly mothers, and so I can call her Father and upset no man. But that is the easy way out: actually it is not quite that simple. In a regrettably precise and dogmatic sense the Christian Church has chosen to say that though God is in all things, and through all things, the first person of the Trinity is most properly called Father. The Church through the centuries has tried to explain this, perhaps most fully in the Athanasian Creed:
>
>> Whosoever will be saved, before all things it is necessary that he hold the Catholic Faith.
>>
>> Which Faith except every one do keep it whole and undefiled, without doubt he shall perish everlastingly.
>>
>> And the Catholic Faith is this: that we worship one God in Trinity, and Trinity in Unity; neither confounding the persons, nor dividing the substance.
>>
>> For there is one person of the Father, another of the Son, and another of the Holy Ghost.
>>
>> But the godhead of the Father, of the Son and of the Holy Ghost, is all one: the Glory equal, the majesty co-eternal . . . So the Father is God, the Son is God and the Holy Ghost is God.
>>
>> And yet there are not three Gods, but one God.[9]

As I do wish to be saved, and do believe that salvation comes through the self-offering of the Son in perfect unity with the Father, through the power of the Holy Spirit, I cannot stop here. This Fatherhood of the first person of the Trinity must be wrestled with, must be claimed back from the pervasive grip of patriarchy, which is one of the powers and dominions that has been cast down and set aside in Christ Jesus.

If we want God to reveal her Fatherhood we must be willing to be children and join a game of dice which Einstein denied God played; a game of chance which the poets know she plays.

She is Father in relation to the tradition. In relation to my tradition. I do not want to stand alone before my God, I am too fearful of the worldly Fathers, too timid and too well-taught. I am dependent on solidarity, in Christ and in the communion of the saints. I want to stand with all my sisters in the faith throughout history. And for them the God they loved, the God who set them free was Father. And in the power of her Fatherhood women of faith, women of Spirit, have found the autonomy and authority to defy the patriarchs who would have kept them in their place as property, as objects, as slaves: Perpetua and Felicity, Margaret of Antioch, Joan of Arc, Clare of Assisi, Hildegard of Bingen, Mary Fisher, Cornelia Connelly—a long and honourable roll-call of the named and the unnamed, who learned from God their Father to defy the fathers and husbands and kings of their world. I'm a white middle-class educated twentieth-century Western woman. The universalist claims of the patriarchs have damaged the world. I want to hear the experiences of other people, from other places and times, and accept the voices of their visions. As a feminist I don't want to claim a universality that I do not have.

And . . . she is Father in relation to me. Her Fatherhood stands over against my sinful desire to create a God in my own image. Mother, I want to say. God is Mother, I want to say, God is like me; God and I are mothers together; *we* understand each other; motherhood is deified in her Motherhood, and so am I. This is sweetness and consolation but I can see the danger of it: I can see it daily in a Church and society in which the generosity of the God who became a man is distorted into the right of men to act like gods; who deny and want to go on denying the Motherhood of God because it undermines their notions of their own divinity. In acknowledging the Fatherhood of God, I acknowledge that God is ultimately Other, the beloved Other; the transcendent, the enormous, the infinite; everything that I'm not, won't become and can't experience, understand or claim to own. Pope John Paul I, in an Angelus address, said 'God is Father. Even more, he is Mother.' And as a woman I have to learn to reverse that. There is a deep way in which it should be natural for men to seek God through female images and women to seek God through male images, because—if we abandoned the projection and denial games—that could become a natural expression of Otherness. But sadly this can't happen while either side of the balanced difference is perceived at any level as being 'better than', 'superior to' or 'more holy than' the other—while the injustice of sexism remains.

And so, believing that God is Father in relation to me, as woman, I am brought back again to my covenant, my commitment to engage in issues of justice and struggle and forgiveness. While contesting the patriarchal forms I still must struggle to recognize and love the God who is my Father, who is infinitely Other to me, who is beyond

and outside of and over and above my little and limited
experience.

And . . . she is, of course, Father in relation to Jesus
Christ, the word made flesh who dwelt among us.

Jesus of Nazareth instructed us, with great simplicity,
to 'Pray without ceasing' and 'when you pray, say "Abba,
Father" '.

When he prayed himself he said 'Father'.

> Father, let this cup pass from me . . .
> Father, let them be one as you and I are one . . .
> Father, forgive them for they know not what they
>   do . . .
> Father, the hour has come; glorify your Son so that
>   your Son may glorify you . . .
> Father, into your hands I commend my spirit.

Quite simply, if 'Father' is good enough for Jesus, surely
it must be good enough for me?

Yes, but it is gift not restriction, it is love not law,
beginning not end; an opening into relationship, not the
slamming of a door. The God without qualities in whom
we believe is too hard for us to love, and in Jesus we are
given generous clues, not prescriptive limitations.

But never forget: 'Not as the world gives, give I unto
you.' God is Father in relation to Jesus, and to us in our
common humanity with Christ, so that Jesus can show us
that she is Father in relation to the patriarchy. 'Call no
man father', he says, 'for you have only one Father, and
he is in heaven. The greatest among you must be your
servant . . . Anyone who exalts himself will be humbled,
and anyone who humbles himself will be exalted.'
Fatherhood, as the ancient earthly power, is to be laid
aside.

Jesus does not tell us to call no woman 'mother'. On

the contrary, he extends the concept of mother beyond the boundaries of biology. He said: 'Anyone who hears the word of God and keeps it is my mother.' For motherhood is without power, without honour, without authority in the world; so the servant God, who has come into the world to set the captives free, will empower motherhood, honour it, and authorize it as in heaven, so on earth.

In God, in her Fatherhood, the fathers of this world are to be set at naught, stripped of their privileges and made into servants. They think they are mighty, but they will be put down from their seats by the God who is almighty, and the poor and the hungry, the humbled and the meek will be exalted.

For God's is no fatherhood as we have learned it from our fathers; it is not a fatherhood of power, but of equality. It is not a fatherhood of authority, but of unity. It is not a fatherhood of domination, of rape and abuse and sexism, but a fatherhood of love. Remember, the Athanasian Creed continues:

So the Father is God, the Son is God and the Holy Ghost is God.
And yet there are not three Gods, but one God.
And in this Trinity none is afore, or after the other;
	none is greater, or less than another;
But the whole three persons are co-eternal together and co-equal.
So that in all things, as is aforesaid, the Unity in Trinity and the Trinity in Unity is to be worshipped.
He therefore that will be saved must thus think of the Trinity.[10]

And in this Trinity none is afore, or after the other; none is greater, or less than another. So we are not talking about any of the fathers we have known.

> She is Father in relation to the patriarchy; she is
> Father so that the power of the Fathers will be broken.
> She is Father in relation to the Trinity so that fathers can
> be given a model of how they ought to be. She is Father
> so that the little ones of the earth—the oppressed, the
> poor, the widows and the orphans—may be set free
> from patriarchy and sing their triumph.

It is in that hope that I use female pronouns; rather than because I believe God is female, which is clearly as ridiculous as suggesting that God is male.

Notes

1. Elizabeth I, speech to the troops at Tilbury on the approach of the Armada (1588): *Oxford Dictionary of Quotations*, p. 206.

2. *Teresa of Avila: The Book of Her Life*, ch. 11; translated by Alison Weber, *Teresa of Avila and the Rhetoric of Femininity* (Princeton University Press, 1990), p. 38.

3. Anyone wishing to know more about Fermat's Last Theorem should consult Keith Devlin, *Mathematics: The New Golden Age* (Pelican, 1988), pp. 177–200.

4. 'The scandal of particularity' is the theological tag for the fact that Jesus—the eternal Logos, that which was with the Father before all worlds, and of whom it can properly be said 'there was not when he was not'—nonetheless became ('folly to the Greeks', to all the philosophers) not 'human' in some abstract sense, but bound, as all human beings are, into a very particular set of circumstances—maleness, Jewishness, first-century-ness, carpenter's-son-ness, etc. It is a useful technical term.

5. Jeremy Taylor, *Ductor Dubitantium*, book II, c. 1, r. 1 and *Works*, vol. XI, p. 485. Cf. Henry McAdoo, *The Spirit of Anglicanism* (A. & C. Black, 1965).

6. Feminists—theological or otherwise—have always had particular difficulties with the dominance of 'logic', as a method of debate, for reasons which I shall discuss in later chapters. This difficulty has led to some particularly creative thinking around methodology and epistemology—cf. for example Mary Grey's *Wisdom of Fools* (SPCK, 1993).

7. Teresa of Avila, *Book of Her Life*, ch. 22, section 8; translated by K. Kavanaugh and O. Rodriguez (ICS, 1988).

8. Francis Thompson, 'In No Strange Land'.

9. Athanasian Creed, Book of Common Prayer translation.

10. Ibid.

1 *Dice throwing made easy*

Stephen Hawking's book *A Brief History of Time*[1] was a commanding international bestseller for several years, which is extraordinary: it is not an easy read. It is not an instant turn-on either (unlike the work of Desmond Morris and Robert Ardrey, authors of *The Naked Ape* and *The Territorial Imperative*, respectively, whose fashionable sociobiology of the 1960s and 1970s fed us—particularly, I have to say, men—an entrancing picture of men as macho heroes, bound by their very genes into an everlasting cycle of aggression and domination: suddenly it wasn't our fault, it was our irresistible baboonish ancestors; Original Sin with no call to repentance, no guilt). Hawking was talking about highly abstract activities, out into the unimaginable distances of space and time which are, it turns out, in any case inseparable. His book is about things not just beyond our language and our concept barriers, but beyond our knowledge boundaries, beyond our common sense and our experience. It describes what might be going on 'out there' beyond the cosmic horizon—that elegant restriction on our sensory knowing, the gift of mystery to be given to future generations. Since nothing can travel faster than light there is a point from beyond which we can receive no sensual information whatsoever: it is too far away for the light or radio impulses etc. to have got here yet. With every passing second the horizon moves out another x million miles as the light finally makes it through the vast vacuity between us and the event. Obviously it is not just a light horizon, but a time horizon too: the longer the universe exists the larger the universe will become for us.

Hawking tried to make it simple for us, but it is not simple and he could not make it so. *A Brief History of Time* is hard work for the average amateur. Yet desire, love even, seems to have driven an extraordinary number of lovers to give it at least their money and so presumably their effort as well.

Science has become fashionable. From a theological point of view it has also become approachable again. While the Newtonian myth of a mechanistic universe, with its reductionist approach, dominated human imagination, there was very little that theology could say. By and large deists and theists together were forced into a relationship with the God of the Gaps, a God who inevitably got smaller and smaller, and so less and less interesting, as the compass of the new mythology extended itself. This was despite the fact that Newton never gave up on his God—his theology was pre-Newtonian, just as Einstein's was to be pre-Einsteinian.

I use the word myth advisedly. The most functionalist and mechanistic of the Newtonians still thought that there was not merely moral good in knowing the Truth, but that their description, their narrative of the universal order was a source of freedom, was a structure and strategy for liberation. When Napoleon asked one of the most famous philosophers of his time, Pierre-Simon Marquis de Laplace, about the place of God in the new scientific universe, Laplace is supposed to have replied 'I have no need of that hypothesis'.[2] 'Supposing', he wrote elsewhere, 'that this being [the intelligent human] were in a position to analyse all events then nothing would be uncertain for him, and both future and past would be open to him.' We would at last be safe from fear.

Given the optimism and arrogance of this science it is not surprising, really, that theology increasingly withdrew into the interior life and a spiritualized private moralism – 'ethics tinged with emotion'. It is not surprising either that things of the spirit were increasingly handed over to women and that they were more and more determinedly shut up within the home – guardians of the domestic shrines, since the intellectual ones had been closed down for the duration. Except for the brave and the stupid, there seemed nothing to do but beat the retreat, and require God to follow the drum. However, the science of this century has, at least at the imaginative level (and it has to be said to the appalled fury of many scientists), reopened the floodgates. Quantum mysticism is trendy; cosmology is chic; dinosaur exhibitions are packed out; the University of Cambridge creates a new job – the Starbridge Lectureship in Theology and the Natural Sciences; the BBC commissions a series in which scientists are asked about their view of the divine;[3] and science fiction is one of the most popular forms of genre fiction available. Speculative theologians, philosophically minded scientists and all sorts of enthusiastic searchers are joining the ranks with enthusiasm.

As I said in the Introduction, I do not look to science to prove or disprove God. From other sources, including of course grace, I know that God IS. I believe in God, as creator, redeemer and sanctifier, as omnipresent, as loving and as powerful. What I want to do then is more modest. Starting from the assumption that God did indeed make the universe, and believing, as I must, that there is a connection, an intimate and sometimes painful connection between what a person *is* and what they do or make, I want only to contemplate what we know of the creation, with a view to asking questions like: What sort of God made this? What can we say about a God who does this? How do we stand in relation to a God who acts so? That is, I want to bring to the study of some of the discoveries of the mathematicians and physicists the same approach as many Christian spiritual and mystical writers (especially Ignatius of Loyola, also fashionable just now) suggest we bring to the Scriptures. God is *here*, we say from a posture of faith. What does this particular *here* have to tell us about God?

The psalmist wrote:

> Understand, O dullest of the people!
> Fools, when will you be wise?
> He who planted the ear, does he not hear?
> He who formed the eye, does he not see?
> He who chastens the nations, does he not chastise?
> He who teaches us knowledge, knows our thoughts.[4]

This psalmist was not engaged in any 'argument by design' exercise. This poet – a better word here than theologian – is not endeavouring to prove that God *exists* as a logical or deductive consequence of ears and eyes existing; the existence of God is a poetic (and theological) certainty to the writer – what is being explored is what we can learn or say about God, because we believe that God created ears and eyes.

My position is similar, but the questions feel a bit trickier. The God who made reverse time in atomic particles, random mutation in therapsids, black holes in the far-flung galaxies, who allows infinity to come in infinite sizes, and oysters to be able to tell the phases of the moon – does this God not . . . *what*? As Paul puts it:

> . . . for the invisible things of him from the creation of the world are clearly seen, being understood by the things that are made, even his eternal power and godhead.[5]

I want to make clear here that I am not trying to, and have little interest in, developing ecological ethics: 'Green is the opiate of the middle classes', as Marx did not say. This does not mean that I don't think ecological considerations should play a more central rôle in our thinking about ethics and particularly thinking about global interdependencies; it means that this is not what I'm wanting to talk about at the moment.

I think that a good deal of contemporary so-called creationist theology has worked itself into a trap by trying to syncretize Christian understandings with certain sorts of pantheism and justify the whole thing in the name of an ecological utopianism which cannot hold water. A lot of this sort of theology is based on a notion which has gained fairly general acceptance, although it seems to me totally unfounded: the unexamined (axiomatic) presupposition that the created world is static and perfect. In order to maintain this presupposition it is necessary to deny that time is real. Plato saw time as an 'accident', as opposed to an essence. In his world of the Ideal there was no time. For the Platonist, of course, the Ideal world *is* the real Real World, while our apparent world is only a shadow, a flickering image of reality. In that real world there will be no time, at least not as an agent of growth, change, movement and so forth. This Platonic desire to ignore the reality of time goes deep in all of us. For example Stephen Hawking, who would be the last to acknowledge this dependency, has been accused by his fellow scientist Ilya Prigogine of trying to eliminate the realness of time as a fundamental and active force of nature, like gravity and thermodynamics and so forth.[6]

Yet such a treatment of the created order is in conflict with the scriptural revelation of time (history) being a creative force in the narrative of redemption, and essential to a meaningful understanding of the Incarnation. 'In the fullness of time' means that the passing of the years, the centuries and the eons has itself created the circumstances of the revelation of God in Christ: this part of the 'scandal of particularity' is often underplayed or even left out. Time, like gravity, is for real and this should not come as a surprise to Christians.

Despite their almost inevitable conflicts, the reason why it is possible for Marxism and Christianity to have a dialogue seems to me to be because, unlike more idealist ideologies, both parties take history, take time with a real seriousness. It seems to me that many current creation theologies do not take time seriously enough; do not take change and growth and death and corruption as the complex realities that they are. Yet time is a force, it is a scientific 'cause' which has effects, results, consequences. The world does not exist outside of time, however much we might like it to.

I do not think that the real problem is with time itself, but with the paucity of our imaginations. God's time-scale is, like God, unimaginably enormous; the mind falters in the face of it, poised on a ghastly chasm of emptiness. It is easier to write off time than to accept the vast vacuity of its expanses. There have not yet been a million *days* since Pentecost and the founding of the Church. 'We're such a young Church', a priest said to me recently when I was complaining about some grossly offensive attempt at Christian articulation, 'a baby Church. You find the early sentences of young children funny and sweet, why can't you be patient?'

'I try to teach my children both grammar and manners', I replied cheekily, but I know what he meant. Christianity is not yet a million days old, although 2,000 years seems almost unimaginable. Yet scientists now call on us to think of the cosmos in thousands of millions of *years*. And since it takes even light a long time to travel the distances involved, miles and years, time and space, become mind-boggingly confused. Distance and time are inextricably entangled, and we find the complexity almost insulting. Our frail intelligences try and simplify the whole thing to make the enormity bearable: we try, ever more desperately to cling to a Platonic sense of being in which time has no real effect.

The neo-classicists of the eighteenth century drew down the curtains of their carriages when they passed over the Alps on their way to Italy so that their elegant sensibilities should not be offended, damaged, by the huge disorderliness of the mountains. Now we admire the mountains, call upon each other to be 'brought down to size' by their magnificent untouchedness, but we treat ourselves in much the same way as they did when we are asked to take on the huge disorderliness of the cosmos. Out there, so long ago we cannot imagine it, in that immeasurable arena stars, whole galaxies, have been born and whirled and died to bring to birth the substance of our bones.

It is all too much. Better to think of a pure still universe untouched by time and sin; and this thing we call time as but a fantasy. Now we see in a glass darkly and the shadow is time, but when we see face to face we'll realize that time did not really count, was extraneous. This is cheating, but we all try it nonetheless.

This business of scale has worried me since I was a child. I had then a collection of tales which included the story of Thumbelina. It was illustrated, and in the pictures Thumbelina, small enough to sleep in a walnut shell, had a long beautiful smooth pigtail. My sister also had a plait of which I was very jealous. This is why, no doubt, the whole thing fixed itself so firmly in my mind – there is always a psychological narrative, plaited in along with the rational narrative, stranded together to make our interests and our selves. Each morning I watched the delicacy with which my mother braided it up. I was never able to understand how Thumbelina's adopted mother, whose fingers were larger than her tiny child's whole body, could manage the manipulation of each individual, nearly invisible, strand. To take my plait image of the Trinity a step further, if an enormous God is trying to plait the divine image onto us like tiny Thumbelinas, it is not surprising that immense amounts of time are needed. The difference in scale is of itself awe-inspiring. Little is gained by trying to eliminate time as part of God's creation: it is not a shadow but an essential, a reality.

In using an idealist model of 'nature', of creation, as the static, time-free, unmoveable zone of God's self-revelation, are we certain that we aren't treating the created order in the same way that we often accuse fundamentalists of treating the Bible, and reactionary Catholics of treating the Church's tradition: that it is inerrant and pre-inscribed? Having learned, painfully, over the last hundred or so years that neither the Bible nor ecclesiology is free from the processes of what it is to exist within time and within the dimensions both of evolution and of sinfulness, we need to be aware that the whole created order may not provide us with an infallible safety-net. The problem is made particularly acute when we remember to bear in mind that we cannot separate ourselves, including our readings and interpretations of scientific descriptions of nature, from the rest of the revelation of God in the creation.

Yet if we can bear it, there are very strong reasons for us to prefer to engage with a dynamic cosmos over a more Thomist or Platonic model. Some of these reasons are quite simply about how the universe *is*, or (at very least) is observed to be, and I shall come on to them later; but there are also good theological reasons. Indeed it is only within a dynamic, historical framework that we can incorporate either political or psychoanalytical understanding of ourselves into a world which is not painfully deterministic, fatalistic. The question I am struggling to ask is whether we can, and should, apply the same sort of thinking to areas beyond the individual, right to the very heart of the creation – the cosmos, matter itself. I believe we can and must in order to preserve our transformatory or revolutionary potential, our claims to be participators in the creation of the Kingdom of God. However this does dislodge us from a cosy retreat which is most easily presented in the form of a classical syllogism:

God made everything and saw that it was good.
God made X (whatever thing we happen to want to
    discuss).
Therefore X is good.

This little trick is always a temptation for any theology of oppression—much feminist and gay liberation theology for example falls, perhaps understandably, into this trap. So, more
arrogantly, do certain New Age theologies, where the earth is
identified not merely as God's but as God. The Gaia principle,
for example, which sees the earth as a living organism (named
after the Greek earth goddess, the Great Mother beloved of
Robert Graves), is a very good example of a lovely poetic
metaphor run wild and turned into a religious principle. The
individual cells of an organism, which is what human beings
become in the Gaia model, cannot personify the organism, let
alone take responsibility for it, as this model requires, without
being given a disproportionate rôle within the organism and
thus slipping neatly back into the anthropocentrism which the
analogy was designed to counteract. The problems proliferate:
Gaia herself is only a fragment, a 'part' of a larger organism
called Cosmos (or some such) or becomes one of a huge
harem of interstellar concubines of the Great God—once
again, one must suppose, male. God is thus reduced to a con-
sort, the annual spouse of the fertility religions, and such re-
duction once again leaves us with a God too small for what the
evidence is offering. The language of analogy works brilliantly
so long, but only so long, as people recognize that it is an
analogy—with all the limitations that analogy is heir to—and
are not dragged into the same sort of literalism (the belief
that what is said completely circumscribes the thing spoken
about) that other fundamentalisms are criticized for.

A still greater danger lies in seeing the earth as somehow
'perfect' and deserving of our worship, even when this
adoration takes the form of devoted and sensitive care. In fact

competition, exploitation, violence and death are at least as real in nature as they are in human institutions. Indeed the human institutions are themselves part and parcel of that creation. Elevating the earth to divine status, with a teaching authority and command over humanity, forces us to be passive before suffering and all too literally brutalized.

A particular version of this theology is seen in the works of Matthew Fox, and because of its popularity I would like to examine it further. As I understand it, the idea goes approximately as follows: We are part of nature and therefore part of God, and so we are good, necessarily and naturally faultless. The problem is the 'institutions' – we can call them 'society' or 'capitalism' or 'sexism' or 'Judeo-Christian culture' or 'heterosexism' or 'materialism' or whatever happens to suit our mood and need of the moment. These institutions somehow impose themselves on our 'true natures' from outside, dulling our individual glory and causing us to do things for which we are then 'forced' to blame ourselves. This makes us feel guilty, which is disagreeable and generally leads to 'bad vibes'. The attraction of such a premise is clear: we can acquit ourselves, cast off tedious and humiliating neurotic Augustinian notions of sinfulness and get on with the delightful task of *self*-realization/actualization/fulfilment, without having to adopt any of the uncomfortable but demanding loneliness that the real disciplined hedonist took on – 'Eat, drink and be merry', without the dangerous and frightening dying tomorrow. This is a cosy place to be – 'wrapped round in earth's diurnal course with rocks and stones and trees',[7] as in the finest cellular cot blanket, bound with satin ribbon. Yet if we are going to accept this baby's comforter, we had better be aware of what we will lose.

Firstly, it is not at all self-evident that everything in the universe is *good* in that sense: I would seriously question the moral virtue of red ants, stinging nettles, the AIDS virus and earthquakes. I would go further and question whether they were actually the pure expression of the will of God. Nor is it clear that we can learn the *goodness* of God simply from looking at X or any other phenomenon. In many cases we certainly can learn about the cleverness, the creativity and wild imagination of God – but loving? tender? nurturing? moral? Even from a human perspective that is simply not what the universe says to us – and from the perspective of the brontosaurus and the dodo the whole show looks like hell on wheels.

In the second place, if we want to justify our own 'I'm OK' blessedness on these slightly flimsy grounds, we will have a hard time challenging anyone else's. Why after all should not prejudice, violence, discrimination and repressive tyranny demand the same affirmation – they exist in the created order, God made the created order and therefore they are good. To claim that everything in the universe, as we see it today, is perfect is to embrace a quietist passivity on both the personal and the social front which is contradictory to the teaching of Scripture and the tradition. For if the creation is exactly as God wants it to be, now and at every minute since the moment of creation, then either Jesus' passion and death become a bizarre blackmail attempt perpetrated by a sick deity, or the conviction that his death had or has meaning is untenable. This goes back to the point that I made in the Introduction: I am looking for a theology, for a description of God, which has transformatory potential, that is effective towards political and social change. A theology that accepts the world as it now is, is not worthy of the God whose bias is towards the poor, the oppressed, the *anawim*, the little ones.

In the third place, all this offers no explanation of how the evil institutions themselves have come into existence. Are they not part of the created order, forged along with sexual conflict in Eden and language at Babel? If they are part of that order then they too ought to be partaking of that created perfection; and if they are not a part of the show along with the rest of us, then there is another force at work, an enormously powerful

35

force – which is other than us, with which we must forever be at war. Does this sound familiar? It sounds like Manichaeism to me: the great dualist heresy which tore the early Church apart. The Manichees attempted to explain the suffering in the world by introducing a second set of powers, over and against us and God. But dualism, in New Age theologies and particularly in Fox, is supposedly the source of all our woes. Perhaps we truly are doomed to repeat our own history – 'the first time as tragedy, the second as farce'.

Fourthly, there is this tricky little number called sin. It has tucked itself into my 'natural' experience at least. I know, as a matter of fact, that on numerous occasions I have sinned: in the simple and old-fashioned sense that I have done things, with as near to free will as I am capable of, even though I knew as I did them that they were not actions of love, solidarity and self-giving. Inasmuch as I wish to delight in my goodness I cannot disown my sinfulness, for if I have no power to act, then my virtue is as institutional as my greed, envy and pride. Even if everyone else is sinless, which I take leave to doubt, my sin alone is enough to skew the vision of us all.

Now I know that volcanoes do not sin, but I do not know that they are not implicated in sin. When Milton was writing *Paradise Lost* it had recently been discovered that the world did not spin on a vertical axis, but was tilted just over 23°. He used this scientific fact in a poetically triumphant metaphor:

> Some say he bid his angels turn askance
> The poles of earth twice ten degrees and more
> Fro the sun's axle; they with labour pushed
> Oblique the Centric globe . . .
>> to bring in change
> Of seasons to each clime; else had the spring
> Perpetual smiled on earth with verdant flowers . . .
> Beast now with beast gan war and fowl with fowl
> And fish with fish; to graze the herb all leaving,
> Devoured each other.[8]

The whole world was changed through sin, was shaken off the true, was tipped sideways forever, which explains the variable seasons, the intemperate zones and rain on the day you've chosen to take a picnic. Without taking an excessively pessimistic Augustinian position on sin, it does not seem unreasonable to me to suggest, as contemporary ecological cosmology would do, that the created order and we, as a part of that order, have an intimate correspondence; and that just as Hitler does not represent God's initial creative impulse, nor does the tsetse fly.[9]

What I am suggesting here is that an honest, open-minded inspection of the creation, intimately including our own selves – with blood on its paws and death in the pot for the living's food – will not reveal directly the sort of God that we might like. For every pretty rainbow and golden sunset there is a child-abuser, a parasitic worm, a senseless randomness, or a lethal power. There is also, more confusingly, a terrible tenderness. It is as much our love as our malice and thoughtlessness that intrude into nature's careless but passionate commitment to change and growth, to evolution. We spare the mutants, treat the infertile, heal the sick, feed the hungry, breed pet dogs, cherish our teddy bears, stalwartly refuse to expose brain-damaged babies on mountain sides. Where does it come from, this dangerous compassion, for we did not learn it from nature, nor from the voracious black holes that spin and suck out there?

Finally, I'd like to suggest that a great deal of contemporary theology working along these lines ends up being deeply functionalist. It has a basic assumption that everything in the created order is *for* some specific purpose and that is why God made it. This tendency is particularly apparent, for fairly obvious reasons, in sexual theology, which I will therefore use as an illustration. Sexuality is so peculiar and unnecessary, the Church seems to have thought, that it must be explained, it must have a purpose, it must be *useful*. Ah, yes, that's easy enough – sex is for procreation. We will carefully overlook the clearly demonstrated fact that God is not *that* unimaginative and has littered the world with examples of procreation without sexual congress just to show what can be done – from the Virgin Birth to self-generating sub-nuclear particles, with the self-dividing amoebae, the hermaphroditic snail and contact-free fish in between.

Unfortunately this way of thinking is deeply infectious. The reflex of theologies that wish to challenge this functionalist view of sexuality is to do so by thinking up some different, but equally functionalist, reasons why God might have created sexual desire.

There are lots of angles you can come at this from, and in fact it is a lot of fun and psychologically quite useful. It is also very easy. From contemporary gay theology I have culled these explicit functions:

(1) Inasmuch as heterosexuality (the expressing of love for that which is Other) models the way a transcendent God loves us, so homosexuality (the expressing of love for that which is Same) models the way in which an immanent, or incarnate, God loves us.

(2) God is a pretty clever creator and wants to demonstrate a capacity for variety and diversity, within the context of love.

(3) The gay community offers us a model for the Church, in that it offers a model of community that is free from evolutionary or functionalist imperatives; a community of love that exists outside of the demands of evolutionary necessity.

(4) God, having foreknowledge, knew about *Humanae Vitae* and wanted to clarify that there was a perfectly good natural method of contraception.

(5) God wanted us to realize that sex was a precious and lovely thing in and of itself, not simply a rather

complicated but sadly necessary means for procreation. Creating pleasurable sexual activity to which this meaning could not be attached is a mark of God's generosity and kindness towards heterosexuals.

. . . and there are indeed a whole lot more.

In fact, these sorts of reasons are probably easier to come up with than theological answers to the question about why God made anyone. Most of the answers to this question are profoundly unsatisfactory. To say that God created us in order to worship him – and I use the masculine pronoun carefully – does not confer much credit on God, whose egomania would seem in this argument rather more pronounced than his love. Alternatively, to argue that God created humanity in order to stop herself feeling lonely rather underrates the personal relationships within the Trinity. Even harder to answer satisfactorily is the still more fundamental question: Why did God make anything *at all*, let alone with the precision and accuracy that seem to have been involved? The best traditional theology seems to come up with here is that God wanted to be a creator, wanted to see if matter was possible . . . but even so . . .

It is actually not difficult to think of satisfying reasons why God might have created homosexuals (or any other sexual orientation). It is, of course, also good fun and psychologically useful and deeply reassuring and consolatory – and I do not see why people should not be consoled and reassured in the face of the homophobia that surrounds us. Nor do I see why homophobic theologians should not have their minds exercised trying to pick holes in any or all of these arguments – it may keep them out of mischief. However I want to suggest that, although perfectly answerable, the question 'Why did God make homosexuality?' – or any other particular phenomenon – is not the right question.

It is a Newtonian, rather than a modern question – it

presupposes the great clock-maker theory of the universe, and reduces God to a craftsperson rather than an artist; and moreover reduces our consciousness, our free will, our incorporation through baptism, and indeed the Incarnation itself to a malicious, or at least absurdist, joke.

In opposition to this presupposition I would like to tell you a story. It is a true story, the story of the horsehair worm.

> The ordained paths of some animals are so rocky as to be preposterous. The horsehair worm in the duck pond, for instance, wriggling so serenely near the surface, is the survivor of an impossible series of squeaky escapes. I did a bit of research into the life cycle of these worms which are shaped exactly like hairs from a horse's tail, and learned that although scientists are not exactly sure what happens to any one species of them, they think it might go something like this:
>
> You start with long strands of eggs wrapped round vegetation in the duck pond. The eggs hatch, the larvae emerge and each seeks an aquatic host, say a dragonfly nymph. The larva bores into the nymph's body where it feeds and grows and somehow escapes. Then, if it doesn't get eaten it swims over to the shore where it encysts on submerged plants. This is all fairly improbable, but not impossibly so.
>
> Now the coincidences begin. First, presumably, the water level of the duck pond has to drop. This exposes the vegetation so that the land host organism can get at it without drowning. Horsehair worms have various land hosts, such as crickets, beetles and grasshoppers. Let's say ours can only make it if a grasshopper comes along. Fine. But the grasshopper had best hurry, for there is only so much fat stored in the encysted worm, and it might starve. Well, here comes just the right species of grasshopper and it is obligingly feeding on shore

vegetation. Now I have not observed any extensive grazing of grasshoppers on any grassy shores, but obviously it must occur. Bingo, then, the grasshopper just happens to eat the encysted worm.

The cyst bursts. The worm emerges in all its hideous length, up to thirty-six inches, inside the body of the grasshopper, on which it feeds. I presume that the worm must eat enough of its host to stay alive, but not so much that the grasshopper will keel over dead far from water. Entomologists have found tiger beetles dead and dying on the water whose insides were almost perfectly empty except for the white coiled bodies of horsehair worms. At any rate, now the worm is almost an adult, ready to reproduce. But first it's got to get out of this grasshopper.

Biologists don't know what happens next. If at the critical stage the grasshopper is hopping in a sunny meadow away from a duck pond or ditch, which is entirely likely, then the story is over. But say it happens to be feeding near the duck pond. The worm perhaps bores its way out of the grasshopper's body, or perhaps it is excreted. At any rate there it is on the grass drying out. Now the biologists have to go so far as to invoke a 'heavy rain' falling from heaven at this fortuitous moment, in order to get the horsehair worm back into the water where it can mate and lay more seemingly doomed eggs. You'd be thin, too.[10]

Pity the poor horsehair worm, and pity even more the vermical theologian who has to wriggle up to a word processor and try to explain to horsehair worms what God's good purpose was in making *them*. Never forget that the God who made the worm made thee.

This is deadly serious. It is true; it is perhaps the Truth. God is not careful, is not bound by the rules. God is careless, profligate even. The imagination of God is outrageous. Annie Dillard goes on to describe God's creativity thus:

> You are God. You want to make a forest, something to hold soil, lock up solar energy and give off oxygen. Wouldn't it be simpler just to rough in a slab of chemicals, a green acre of goo? . . . In other words even at the perfectly ordinary and clearly visible level creation carries on with an intricacy unfathomable and apparently uncalled for. The first ping into being of the first hydrogen atom *ex nihilo* was so unthinkable, so violently radical, that surely it should have been enough, more than enough. But look what happens. You open the door and all heaven and hell breaks loose. And evolution, of course, is the vehicle of intricacy . . . this is the truth of the pervading intricacy of the world's detail: the creation is not a study, a roughed-in sketch; it is supremely meticulously created; created abundantly, extravagantly and in fine . . . Look at practically anything – the coot's feet, the mantis' face, a banana, the human ear – and see that not only did the creator create everything, but that he is apt to create *anything*. He'll stop at nothing. There is no-one standing over evolution with a blue pencil to say, 'Now that one there is absolutely ridiculous and I won't have it.' If the creature makes it, it gets a stet. Is our taste so much better than the creator's? The creator creates. Does he stoop, does he speak, does he save, succour, prevail? Maybe. But he creates. He creates everything and anything.[11]

It is terrifying. God plays preposterous games. God allows complexity, encourages complexity. God obliges us to play the game of becoming, and does not permit us to rest on her laurels but to go on making things new, making new things.

Having thus snatched away the creationist safety-net as I

warned, we are left with a deep long view. We have to struggle to replace a functionalist, bureaucrat God with an artist God – that is to say a God who loves both beauty and risk. The goodness of God may be hard to argue from the creation – the flamboyance, the abundance, the sheer ebullience of God however is not. The generosity of a God who can create a universe so highly complex, so intricate, so random that there can be reverse time in the atom, and diversity of sexuality in the human, and death among the far-flung stars is a generosity that should encourage not only gratitude but awe. All those things are essential to what it is to know God. God's willingness to run risks for the sake of a risky delight should boggle our minds; and just in case our stubborn minds fail to be boggled we also have a God generous enough to run the yet more bizarre risk of entering into that created order.

If we are going to allow God to give us the gift of knowing God through the creation, if we are going to allow ourselves to receive this aspect of revelation, it seems to me that we need to listen harder to the people whose job it is to find out what is going on there. That is the scientists – physicists and mathematicians, and the life scientists as well. Fred Hoyle, a contemporary physicist, wrote once:

> I have always thought it curious that while most scientists claim to eschew religion, it actually dominates their thoughts more than it does the clergy.[12]

I'm afraid this may be true. If it is, it may explain why so many non-scientists are frightened of science; are convinced that scientists are trying to steal our magic away from us and replace it with a hi-tech refrigerated universe. From the beginning of the nineteenth century, probably starting with Mary Shelley's wonderful *Frankenstein*, European culture has regarded science and particularly technology – applied science – as the immensely powerful enemy, fighting to undermine the lovely eccentricities and charm of human beings and replace them with robots. *Brave New World* carries this myth forward, but so – more interestingly – do the highly violent comics, films and video games of contemporary popular culture where cyborgs, cloned mutants, half-humans and computerized robots struggle to take over the world. The contemporary hero adopts direct physical violence as a means to compete; while the villains of this literature sit in dark places and manipulate machinery. I suggest that a great deal of this odd mind-set, which sees technical progress as necessarily threatening and keeps on indulging in nostalgic utopias, has been brought about by a Christianity which has understood human cleverness as being opposed to God. 'Be good, sweet maid, and let who will be clever' seems to have its roots in a misplaced fear that intellect and virtue are incompatible.

Certainly scientism seems to be 'winning' over religiosity in our current society, but that may be because we, the Christian community, have made a horrible error about science: an error based in arrogance which itself creates the necessary conditions for the opposing arrogance of scientists. Why should they have respect for so stupid a viewpoint? This conviction that human ingenuity will reduce the influence of God seems to me to grow, once again, out of that fundamental dualism which supposes that matter is somehow less God's than 'spirit' is.

The mediaeval Church regarded theology as the Queen of sciences: the ordering, interpreting force which gave rhythm and harmony to the pursuit of knowledge. This is a lovely rich image, and the cosmological scientists of the time responded lovingly with a world-view that went something like this:

God made the universe in seven days. At the centre of it, the apple of its father's eye, hung the earth, tiny but beloved and lovely. Around it in harmonious unity spun the spheres, singing as they danced, serving it for light and warmth and rest and joy. And this jewel was itself only the setting for God's creation of Man: the pinnacle of God's achievement, made in God's image, given dominion over all the creatures. Every last detail of the whole order of nature was made carefully and lovingly by God for the use of God's favourite creation, God's children – herbs for *his* health, animals for *his* food, wine for *his* joy, women for *his* helpers, and almost everything for *his* edification and education. The world abounded in symbols and signs deliberately made by God to remind and assist Man in the search for his true homeland in heaven.

Thus the robin's breast is red to remind us of Christ's passion.

Rocks are hard to remind us of the toughness of Peter (and the power of the papacy).

Pelicans cut their own breasts to feed their young with their blood so that we shall be reminded (on the presumably infrequent occasions when we happen to encounter a nesting pelican) of God's suffering love for us all.

And we were given ten fingers so that we could say the rosary even if we had left our beads at home!

> We can hardly imagine a state of mind in which all
> material objects were regarded as symbols of spiritual
> truths or episodes in sacred history. Yet, unless we make
> this effort of imagination, mediaeval art is largely
> incomprehensible.[13]

This is an elegant and eloquent world-view, comforting and beautiful. I don't believe a word of it, and nor do you, but forget that for the moment. The Church liked it a lot, and who could blame her? It made humanity singularly important, and it gave the Church enormous authority. The trouble was she liked it too well. Whenever it was called into question the Church took immediate action to prevent such dangerous heresies from being circulated. Eventually in 1663 Galileo turned up saying something like 'Sorry gang, but I have been looking through this little telescope thing, which I have invented, at what God's cosmos actually is doing. And, I've got news for you: Ptolemy was wrong, Copernicus was right; we haven't got a geocentric universe.' Did the theological authorities of his day say 'Wow! You mean, God is even cleverer than we thought'? Did they say 'Thank you, for giving us something to work on, something that will reveal yet more of the divine to us'? Did they even say 'Are you sure?' No, they said 'Shut up or we'll kill you'.

This still goes on. Galileo's condemnation marked a turning point in Christian history which is tragic and we are still all living in the light of that tragedy. *Eppur si muove*, legend says he muttered as he signed his recantation, 'but still it *does* move'. He was a man more obedient to the Church's authority than the Church's authorities were. A man saying as Boff said when condemned more recently, 'I would rather walk together with my Church than alone with my theology' – and neither of them asking why they should have to make so idiotic a choice. Theology, the mediaeval Queen of the sciences, abdicated at that moment from a beautiful and spacious realm, ever since has been huddled inside a sealed fortress, suffering from delusional paranoia and terrified of the destructive and marauding hoards of vandals supposedly ravaging out there; scared brainless of the discoveries of science. To make sure that not too many people pay too much attention to the scientists they have been villainized in particularly subtle ways (much as women have), and too many of us have fallen victim to our own bogeyman.

One little example, although there are many, will demonstrate just how terrified honest and intelligent Christians can be about scientific descriptions of reality. In the nineteenth century scientists began to read the fossil record in a new way. It became increasingly clear that species not mentioned in the Bible really had lived and had become extinct. This was well before Charles Darwin discovered evolution by random

mutation and subsequent selection – and, hence, had con-
ceived the idea that we might share common ancestors with
other primates – so the threat to human dignity, if it was a
threat, was fairly minimal. Nonetheless in defence of the
Genesis account of the creation the argument was put forward
and widely accepted that when the world was being created in
the six days outlined in Genesis, God had deliberately
implanted the odd fossil bone here and there *in order to test the
faith of nineteenth-century divines*. This does seem to me to be
perverse in the most technical sense of that word: to find
reducing God to the intellectual level of a silly schoolboy
preferable to admitting that the Genesis account was more
complex than had been expected.[14]

Teresa of Avila, who was not a lady to scare easily, uses a
certain delicate sarcasm to attack the terror of the physical
world in the hierarchies of her time:

> This withdrawal from the corporeal world must
> doubtless be good, since it is advised by such spiritual
> people, but my belief is that it should be practised only
> when the soul is very proficient; until then it is clear that
> the Creator must be sought through the creatures.[15]

The sad thing about all this is not simply that we make
ourselves ridiculous. As an example of the ridiculous I would
instance the refusal to face up to the damaging evidence of
embryo research, which smashes real holes in the argument of
ensoulment at conception. Take the development of identical
twins for example: several days after the merger between the
ovum and the sperm, the gamete (a technical word for the
foetus at this point) divides arithmetically, but is completely
unified. All the cells in this gamete are completely unspecified
– they can develop into any particular cell function (tissue,
organs, bones etc.); you can even remove and destroy some or
most of these cells and the foetus will continue to develop

normally. This is, according to the tradition, a complete and unique human being, possessing a complete and unique soul. Then, quite randomly, this gamete splits and two embryos develop. What theologically is held to have happened? Did the soul split in two? Impossible, the soul is indivisible. Did a new soul appear? Impossible, the child had a soul from the moment of conception. Is one of the resulting twins soul-less? Impossible, obviously. Could it just possibly be not that the idea of uniqueness is wrong but that the language in which we express it, 'ensoulment from the moment of conception', is hopeless – in the straightforward sense that the theory is not consonant with the experimental data?

The real sadness is not that we cause people to laugh at the idea of God and alienate them from the source of their very selves – God can almost certainly cope with that, although it is a pity – but that we deprive ourselves of revelation, of knowledge of God.

Natural history is not taught in seminary. This is curious, since most people in pastoral ministry are about 435 times more likely to be asked about cosmology or sub-nuclear physics or evolution or 'the argument from design' than they are to be asked about Greek irregular verbs or the dangers of patripassianism. The question 'Why not?' has to be asked. 'Maker of heaven and earth' is the first credal statement; it is not unreasonable to require professional Christians to know at least something about what that heaven and earth actually *are*.

The funny thing is that many scientists, and particularly those dealing with cosmology, subatomic physics and mathematics, do do theology to a quite extraordinary degree. This may be because they have nothing to be scared of. Stephen Hawking, for example, is certainly not scared or ashamed to deal with such issues. He openly believes his science has displaced God entirely – or as he puts it:

The idea that space and time may form a closed surface without boundary also has profound implications for the rôle of God in the affairs of the universe. With the success of scientific theories in describing events, most people have come to believe that God allows the universe to evolve according to a set of laws and does not intervene in the universe to break those laws. However the laws do not tell us what the universe should have looked like when it started – it would still be up to God . . . So long as the universe had a beginning, we could suppose it had a creator. But if the universe is really completely self-contained, having no boundary or edge, it would have neither beginning nor end: it would simply be. What place then for a creator?[16]

Nor is he alone; there are still many scientists who would say of God, as Laplace did, 'I have no need of that hypothesis'. Or in more contemporary terms, as Angela Tilby reports Dr Jonathan Miller saying when she consulted him about her TV series *Soul*, that they regard religion as a form of mental illness.[17] God no more forces faith on astrological physicists and mathematicians than on the rest of us.

Nonetheless looking for the scientific facts among the far-flung astral bodies, just as peering at them within the whizzing orbits of the atom, seems to affect people's language and therefore we may assume their consciousness. Elsewhere in the same book Hawking, who can imagine no 'point' in a creator, no place or need for one, demands in painfully beautiful and urgent terms, which seem more reminiscent of the Spanish mystics than of deductive logic,

> What is it that breathes fire into the equations and makes a universe for them to describe?[18]

Many contemporary scientists, and particularly those working

49

on the outer boundaries of the imagination—with things that are inconceivably small or unimaginably vast—are less arrogant even than this. Scientists come to the questions of ultimate meaning with carefully trained minds, more disciplined in clarity perhaps than anyone else nowadays. They come to these questions also with an open-mindedness of a special sort, as their trade requires it of them. All theory must be submitted to the process of experiment, and all experiment must be repeatable. Even when they report back as nonbelievers it seems to me that they bring us the precious gifts of epiphany, magi from a distant land bearing gold, frankincense and myrrh.

I am not now going to drag you through a quick guided tour of post-Einsteinian physics, nor modern mathematics, nor contemporary biology. This is mainly because I do not know enough about them. If you want to try your hand at finding God's revelation in this way there are some excellent books. *The Mind of God* by Paul Davies,[19] the Professor of Mathematical Physics at the University of Adelaide, addresses the issue directly. Keith Devlin's *Mathematics: The New Golden Age*[20] does everything it can to help non-mathematicians understand the issues. Angela Tilby's *Soul*[21] creates a direct investigative dialogue between some of the most exciting contemporary scientists and an orthodox Christianity.

What I am going to do is tell you a few little stories, which show that scientists, far from pushing us into an apologetic God-of-the-Gaps sheepishness, are in fact opening up for us a vision of God infinitely greater, bigger, cleverer, wilder than our somewhat stunted imaginations have allowed us; a God who is not tamed and constricted by our definitions; a God who challenges us.

Most of these stories are contemporary stories.

Until the beginning of the nineteenth century mathematics was held to relate, absolutely, to the real world. Its starting point was Euclid and his geometry, whose axioms had been worked out in what would now be called 'lived experience'. He drew diagrams in the sand and then worked out principles to explain what was and what was not drawable — on these principles his mathematics was based and accepted more or less universally, by those who cared. This conviction did more than undergird mathematics itself; it was widely influential in developing principles, government, art and behaviour. For example, Kant's philosophy was wedded to the inevitability, the concrete truth of Euclid's geometry. For him it was the central example of his a priori knowledge system, which depends on some things being *necessarily* true: the way we were as thinking human beings, the way our brains were constructed, guaranteed that we would find Euclid's axioms solidly and unshakably true.

However during the nineteenth century mathematicians had begun to work with non-Euclidean geometries. They found not just that Euclid's model, the supposed touchstone of absolute logical certainty, was by no means an inevitable and 'true' description of how the world really was, but that it was not even, in some circumstances, the best description. There was a whole range of different geometries available. For example, the Euclidean theories assume, sometimes implicitly, that all space is flat.[22] In flat space, of course, parallel lines never meet and the three internal angles of a triangle always add up to 180°. Whereas — as Einstein proved conclusively in 1915, but as other mathematicians had already speculated — in reality not all space is flat: parallel lines can meet and triangles get up to all sorts of tricks. On the surface of a sphere, for instance, there is a completely different geometry not only possible but necessary.[23] This discovery undermined idealist thinking about the world in a profoundly radical way, and opened the door wide for more contemporary relativism and empiricism.

Geometry, throughout the seventeenth and eighteenth

centuries, remained, in the war against empiricism, an
impregnable fortress of the idealists. Those who held –
as was generally held on the Continent – that certain
knowledge, independent of experience, was possible
about the real world, had only to point to geometry:
none but a madman, they said, would throw doubt on its
validity and none but a fool would deny its objective
reference.[24]

In the face of this loss of their citadel many mathematicians
fled in exile from the 'real' and came increasingly to regard
their science in a highly formalist way: a creation, an invention, of the highest organizational, logical capacities of the
human mind. Even if it had no reference to the outside world
it remained in and of itself a pure and beautiful construct of
perfect deductive reasoning; a head game, but a lovely one.

Alas, the deconstruction of mathematics did not stop here.
On 8 August 1900, in Paris, at the Second International
Congress for Mathematicians (which had, incidentally, been
rearranged so that it would fall in the opening year of the new
century, a curiously sentimental decision for such rigorous
logicians to indulge themselves with), David Hilbert, a 38-
year-old professor from the University of Göttingen and one
of the leading mathematicians of the time, gave the keynote
speech. It was a dynamic and forward-looking speech, which
has rightly become famous. Instead of looking back at the
extraordinary mathematical success of the nineteenth century, he outlined 23 significant unsolved mathematical problems which needed to be tackled, and summed up the position
with sweeping optimism:

> We hear within us the perpetual call: there is the
> problem. Seek its solution. You can find it by reason, for
> in mathematics there is no *ignorabimus* (we will not
> know).[25]

One of these problems was to discover a general procedure for proving mathematical theorems: which means, to put it simply, to establish a logical method for deciding in a finite number of steps whether a given mathematical statement was true or false. Following Hilbert's rhetorical lead nobody at the time doubted that such a procedure did exist—there was indeed no *ignorabimus*—it was just a matter of finding it and proving it. Thirty years later, with two startlingly simple (in mathematical terms) theorems, Kurt Gödel proved conclusively that it was demonstrably impossible to prove any such thing.

By the turn of the century, in contemporary mathematics the formalists would seem to have won: Hilbert's invitation to give the crucial address represented that victory. He, like most mathematicians at that point, believed that all mathematics could be regarded as the formal logical manipulation of symbols based on prescribed axioms. All that was needed were axiom systems that were complete and consistent. What Gödel demonstrated, using the formal rules of mathematics, was that in any axiom system there will always and necessarily be relevant statements that can be neither proved nor disproved from those axioms (The First Incompleteness Theorem). Worse still, from the point of view of Hilbert's project, among the unprovable statements is the statement that the axiom system is consistent (The Second Incompleteness Theorem).

This does not, of course, mean that the axiomatic approach to mathematics falls apart on the instant and can be used no more; it does mean that the all-conquering stride of calculation, of logical mathematics was found to have limits. The awareness of those limits has increased, rather than diminished, ever since.

Gone for ever is the old expectation that, given enough time and ingenuity, any 'genuine' problem in mathematics could be resolved one way or the other. Besides the true statements and the false statements there is a third class: undecideable statements, statements which cannot be proven to be either true or false.[26] This is not a little quirky corner of mathematical logic; the problem of self-reference, as the logical hole is called, is substantial:

> Undecideable propositions run through mathematics like threads of gristle that criss-cross a steak in such a dense way that they cannot be cut out without the entire steak being destroyed.[27]

To understand why this is so devastating a discovery it is necessary to understand what mathematics purports to be. Mathematical proof is of a different kind from other scientific truths, which are acceptably proved by experiment, by the conformity of the theory to the material, experienced, physical world – the world itself is the ultimate judge of the truth or otherwise of the idea. But mathematics had made greater claims — it dealt with abstracted, pure ideals. How much this is the case can be seen from the very nature of numbers. They are abstractions, ideals: the number 3 cannot be separated from three-ness. Nothing in the material world is 3, it is just a symbolic expression of what certain sizes of groups of disparate objects have in common. (What is truly amazing is how quickly small children can see what three balls, three boys and the funny wiggly sign '3' have in common.) 3 is an agreed sign given to this abstract nothing.

The only way to make these abstractions remotely useful or intelligible is to lay down some ground rules – some axiom systems which say how you can play with the abstractions (2 + 2 *will* equal 4). However if these axiom systems cannot be proved to be complete or consistent (or, can be proved not to be complete and consistent) the acceptance of mathematical methodology becomes an act of faith. Even simple little sums – like insisting that 8 + 1 will always equal the same as 1 + 8 – are huge steps in the dark, are indeed leaps of faith. In fact, in life we know that this is often not true: when getting dressed in the morning we know that the order in which we add socks and shoes to our body makes a very noticeable difference to the end result. Or, as John Barrow, a mathematical historian has commented, 'If a religion is defined to be a system of thought which requires belief in unprovable truths, then mathematics is the only religion that can prove it is a religion'.[28]

This need not alarm us as Christians; we have always known that the infinite could not be proven by logic alone, because our faith is revealed, is gift. Yet it is exciting to think that when God laid down the deep laws, the laws of the physical universe, they revealed in their patterned depths exactly what is also revealed in the Scriptures and the tradition. Faith is a radical act because we *choose* what we will believe; the most basic axioms of mathematics, for example the commutative law of addition or the associative law of addition, are acts of faith. They are no more provable than the existence of God, but numbers like God are infinite. So there is choice – there is nothing proven – and where there is choice there is obligation to choose, so that faith is a radical act because it is an act of choosing. Contemporary scientism has to recognize this; just as contemporary theism has had to recognize that God cannot be 'proven' logically and must be instead received joyfully and gratefully.

When Gödel challenged mathematical certainty he was doing so within a recognized philosophical debate: mathematicians have always been divided as to whether they were inventors or discoverers. It is a delicate and important difference: Cortes, from his peak in Darien, *discovered* the Pacific – it had always been there; James Watt, on the other hand, *invented* the steam engine – until he made it, it was not. Or, to put it another way, Freud discovered the subconscious, and invented psychoanalysis. The distinction is not in fact always clear and simple, though it is often imaginatively rich.

What Gödel did was to make untenable the belief that mathematics was strictly only a human invention: if that was all it was, it was not much use since it could not guarantee its own coherence.

Many mathematicians, like Hilbert, felt that the self-sufficiency of mathematics was its central glory.

('What's the difference between maths and physics?' I asked a mathematician recently. 'If it's for anything, or about anything, it isn't maths', she replied.)

Despite Gödel, however, many mathematicians go on believing that they are inventors – that their theorems have no external point of reference; and they are happy to be playing a game. Others however take a more Platonic position; that, as James Jeans once put it, 'God is a mathematician'. Following Galileo, who declared that 'the book of nature is written in mathematical language', some mathematicians believe that there is a real meaning to the 'unreasonable effectiveness of mathematics in the natural sciences', that 'it is probable that there is some secret here which remains to be discovered'.[29]

Nonetheless, because of the highly abstract and formal nature of mathematics, Gödel's Incompleteness Theorems – while they threw up massive methodological problems for mathematicians – did not obviously undermine the mechanistic, reductionist project of a knowable world. Scientists, particularly physicists, could still have faith that it would be possible to discover the past and future, by knowing the present position of everything and the rules by which things changed; a world that had been fixed and determined at the outset because everything, from the very smallest particle of matter to the whole cosmos, was driven by immutable laws, and these were accessible to human intelligence.

In the 1920s quantum physics put paid to that grandiose dream, once and for all. The best known expression of that mortal wound is Werner Heisenberg's Uncertainty Principle. Heisenberg proved, to the satisfaction of almost everyone who can understand it (and I have to admit I am not one of them), that

> All measurable quantities (e.g. position, momentum, energy, time) are subject to unpredictable fluctuations in their values. This unpredictability implies that the micro-world is indeterministic.[30]

That is just the beginning. The Uncertainty Principle does not mean only that you cannot predict what is going to happen next, you cannot even describe accurately what is happening now. Heisenberg proved that the more tightly you focus on one of a pair of measurements, the vaguer the other necessarily becomes — it is impossible to know with any degree of accuracy at all both where a subatomic 'thing' is *and* how fast it is going somewhere else. Speed or position; one or the other, but not both – not now, not ever.

Let us be clear, or at least as clear as possible. In the first place this is true at the subatomic level and at the material level – at the macro level, the level of sensory perception and getting-on-with-lifeness, Newtonian physics and the laws of cause and effect work perfectly well. There remains a scientific problem about how a quantum-level Big Bang, produced out of a time-and-space-smeared quantum singularity (as current theory-of-origin orthodoxy teaches), has generated macro-level, 'Newtonian' phenomena, including us and our capacity to care about any of this.

There is no quick high-board dive off a stable mechanistic platform into a chaotic lawless ocean – Bohr, Heisenberg and their colleagues do not suggest this. The uncertainties are firmly bounded by probabilities: either the particle will leap, say, from one orbit to another, or it won't; we don't know which but we do know it will do one or the other and can calculate the odds. Schrödinger's poor abused cat will be either dead or alive – it won't have turned into a mouse. This is not alchemy or magic. Within the subatomic world, out of which the macro world is unquestionably made, there is no deterministic teleological power at work. There is randomness and chance. Randomness, like determinism, shapes how the world will be tomorrow, but it does it quite differently. Matter, at least at this level, is itself at high risk, creative. Time is not just the unfolding, the reading off, of an already written text, a mere turning of the pages; it is an active, creative force that cannot, of its nature, be predicted. It is a force, like gravity or electromagnetism, that creates the parameters of change and thus participates in the coming into being of some completely new thing. New things happen whose causes are not. Not just are not known but are not existent, until chance brings them into existence.

John Wheeler, an eminent physicist, tells a lovely little parable about 'how it is' or at least seems to be; how the combination of chance and law works in the making of things. He was once involved in a game along the lines of 'Animal, Vegetable, or Mineral'. Only 'yes/no' answers could be given to his questions and he had to work out what object the group had selected. At first his questions were answered very promptly, but gradually the responses seemed to get slower and more thoughtful. Finally, blindly, he jumped. 'Is it a cloud?' he asked. 'Yes', the other players all said, and laughed. Then they admitted that they had not thought of any word at all, but had answered his questions at random, with the sole proviso that there should be no contradictions. The 'right' answer would be the first one that he came up with that did not contradict their answers. Thus, within the laws of their game, his questions and their random, but boundaried, replies had *created* the answer – from an initially almost infinite, chaotic range of possibilities.

If this is how it is – and it seems more confusing to argue the case than to accept it – then there are theological consequences. It was these that Einstein could not accept: 'The

Old Man does not throw dice', he insisted. Yet here in the quantum world, and therefore in the world which we inhabit, God does throw dice, God is a gambler. There is risk at the heart; and God, bolder than we are, consents to that risk. God has built risk in, has created things thus, so that, not merely at the moral and individual level but at the cosmic level, the creation can participate in its own creativity.

God may of course still be unmoved and omnipotent, but in the great act of creation at least that is not the characteristic that God chooses to reveal. We have a God more generous than that – more faithful, more trusting, more responsive. In fact we have a God very much more like the one the writers of the Hebrew Scriptures tried to speak of. A God of history, of time, and of self-giving. A God of love.

I shall tell you only one more story about the world as these contemporary explorers describe it. At the end of the nineteenth century, the mathematician Georg Cantor proved that infinity comes in different sizes. There are larger and smaller infinities.

I find this an extraordinarily delightful piece of information. I have to admit that my delight has a personal element: Cantor's proof was the first mathematical theory that I felt I understood. I mean not that I believed its results, but that imaginatively and creatively I could follow the argument. It was for me a breakthrough – I went around grinning like a maniac for several days; I even had a character in my last novel explain the proof to her sister.[31]

Earlier in this chapter I quoted Hoyle saying that while most scientists claim to eschew religion, it actually dominates their thoughts. Nowhere is this more true than when it comes to infinities. Scientists love infinity, unlike Christians who tend to shy away from the idea like nervous ponies – stressing immanence and Christology at all costs. Even 'soft' scientists like economists love the idea of infinities: it makes their work so much more elegant. For despite its total abstraction, the infinite is a world of great simplicity. Going from the finite to the infinite is very much like stepping back from a television screen: when you are far enough away, the indecipherable complexity of the large number of tiny light dots occupying the screen is recognized as a coherent picture. By going to the infinite, the complexity of the very large finite is lost.

Cantor showed mathematicians how to play in the world of the infinite. It was the loveliest treasure he brought back from his pioneering adventure into the world of set theory (which underlies the way math is taught in primary schools now). Bertrand Russell described Cantor's achievement as 'possibly the greatest of which the age can boast'. While David Hilbert – yes, the same optimistic formalist whom we met earlier – boasted 'from the paradise created for us by Cantor, no one will drive us out'.[32]

Most infinities are the same size as each other; that is, the items in one infinity can be matched to, paired off with, the items in another. (For example, an infinite list of natural numbers will be the same size as an infinite list of prime numbers.) Initially all that Cantor's proof showed was that the power set (that is, the set consisting of all the sub-sets) of an infinite set was larger than the infinite set. Yet that is enough. From a theological point of view it is more than enough – it is grace abounding. In fact, in 1963 Paul Cohen, an American mathematician, using a new logical technique called forcing, proved that there is an infinite range of infinities. Paul Davies assures us:

> We cannot know Cantor's Absolute [which is the
> mathematical name for the largest possible infinity], or
> any other Absolute by rational means, for any Absolute
> being a Unity and hence complete within itself, must
> include itself . . . if it is a One, then it is a member of
> itself, and thus can only be known through a flash of
> mystical vision. . . . We are barred from ultimate

knowledge, from ultimate explanation, by the very rules of reasoning that prompt us to seek such an explanation in the first place. If we wish to progress beyond, we have to embrace a different concept of 'understanding' from that of rational explanation.[33]

So when I speak of a 'Big-Enough God' I am not merely speaking of an infinite God but of the God of infinities, the Absolute which either chooses to reveal itself or remains veiled in mystery.

There is, you see, nothing to be afraid of even in the rarefied world of pure science. In the very limits of logic and the outer reaches of knowable time and space, in the heart of the Big Bang itself, in the springing into being of the first hydrogen atom *ex nihilo*, there is immeasurable infinity, there is the unknowable Absolute – and contemporary science proves it, by the most rigorous methods we can discern. Nor need we fear, as I think there is a tendency to do, that 'hard' scientific knowledge will strip away beauty, any more than it will destroy mystery. Increasingly science recognizes the rôle that beauty – usually called 'elegance' by mathematicians – plays in the discernment of truth.

> Mathematics, rightly viewed, possesses not only truth but supreme beauty – a beauty cold and austere, like that of sculpture.[34]

> The mathematician's patterns, like the painter's or the poet's, must be *beautiful*, the ideas, like the colours or the words must fit together in a harmonious way. Beauty is the first test; there is no permanent place in the world for ugly mathematics . . . It may be very hard to define mathematical beauty, but that is just as true of beauty of any kind – we may not know quite what we mean by a

> beautiful poem, but that does not prevent us from
> recognizing one.[35]

What Keats said about art: 'Beauty is truth, truth beauty'; and Isaiah said about life: 'Beautiful on the mountains are the feet of them who bring good news'; is the same thing as scientists are saying about their own work.

You may be thinking that this does not get us very far. We have lost a knowable world. We have lost a servile science and an all-powerful deity. In exchange all I am offering you is a wild immeasurability, and a God who seems prepared to let the whole thing go its own chaotic and random way. However I am certain that accepting all of this randomness and unknowability gives us more, if we dare to receive it, than it takes away. I believe what we have gained is complexity, freedom and loveliness. We have gained a universe so extraordinary that it should stun us into awe, and a God so magnificently clever and creative that we can have confidence in such a creator's ability to sort out tiny little problems like the resurrection of the body without too much trouble. We are shown a universe that can keep us on our toes, agog with excitement.

We need just such a wide-eyed wonder to keep us in our place; and our place is the infinite cosmos which the still more infinite God has given us. Really given, not just lent; given in the sense that we are both allowed and obliged to create it, to create genuinely new things, new possibilities within it. 'A universe is forever, not just for Christmas.' The ground of our hope is God's delight and confidence in matter itself, and us as part of it.

I would like to suggest that the division, the competition we have set up between God as creator and God as law-giver, or in its more lovable form God as redeemer, is unsound and dangerous. For a start it is damaging to the fullness of the trinitarian concept; in an odd sense Christianity has become

excessively Christocentric. We need to get back to the extraordinary imagination and power of God, as creator, to regain
a balance.

> In the beginning God created.
> In the beginning God created heaven and earth.
> In the beginning God created heaven and earth and saw
>   that it was good.
> Before God redeemed, God made.

Of course the philosophic impasse remains: how can a
necessary and infinite God create a contingent and evolving
cosmos? I don't logically know the answer to this, but I'm not
too bothered given the extraordinary universe in which we
live. Even the failure to be able to discover a logically coherent
process here is alleviated by one of the developments of post-
Einsteinian physics. Bohr's Theory of Complementarity
shows us not that something can be two things at once but that
two incompatible discourses can be needed to understand or
describe something:

> The language of quantum theory is precise but tricky.
> Quantum theory does not state that something – like
> light for instance – can be wave-like and particle-like *at
> the same time*. According to Bohr's Complementarity, light
> reveals either a particle-like or a wave-like aspect
> depending on the context (i.e. the experiment). It is not
> possible to observe both the wave-like aspect and the
> particle-like aspect in the same situation. *However, both
> these mutually exclusive aspects are needed to understand 'light'*.
> In this sense light is both particle-like and wave-like.[36]

Given the close symbolic connection made between God and
light, this idea of complementarity may help us imaginatively
to consent to a God who is powerful *and* generous; who is

63

transcendent *and* immanent; who is three persons *and* one God.

I do not need to be able to explain God, only to look at the works of that mighty power, accepting all their complexity and ingenuity, and be impressed, enchanted, awed. When we feel in need of more explanation we need think only of that moment when we see another human being and find in them the delineations of beauty, the possibility of love and delight. For at that moment we act as God acts to the whole of creation: it is not for anything – it is beauty, delight, joy, fun, creativity. It is love.

This seems to me to be, in part, an answer to the underlying questions, the key questions. Why did God create *this* universe? Why did God create *anything at all*? Or as Dillard, whom I quoted earlier in this chapter, puts it:

> Creation carries on with an intricacy unfathomable and apparently uncalled for. The first ping into being of the first hydrogen atom *ex nihilo* was so unthinkable, so violently radical, that surely it should have been enough, more than enough. But look what happens. You open the door and all heaven and hell breaks loose.[37]

This is the great mystery, but it need not be perplexing or worrying. If the cosmos, matter itself, exists in love, rather than for some bureaucratic or edifying purpose, it can, indeed it must, be free to grow, develop, evolve, change, experiment – profligately, extravagantly, randomly. The first ping into being of the first hydrogen atom *ex nihilo*, unthinkable and violently radical though that was, cannot be enough for love – any more than looking at your newborn baby, or spotting someone seriously fanciable at a party can be enough: you desire the thing or person you love to display more and more of what it is to be what they are in the process of becoming, to change and grow and respond. It is only in the context of this extraordinary activity that we can truly rejoice in the genero-sity of our God; that we can live free from fear; that we can choose love and participation and joy; that we can realize what we have truly been given.

We are justified through faith not works – and I speak not of our faith but of God's faith in imagination and creativity, and hence in the developing weirdness of creation. Unlike the rest of us, God has no ethical imperatives. Art for art's sake is a divine prerogative.

Notes

1. Stephen Hawking, *A Brief History of Time* (Bantam Books, 1988).
2. Laplace, quoted in Paul Davies and John Gribben, *The Matter Myth* (Viking, 1991), p. 27.
3. Angela Tilby's programme *Soul*, also available as a BBC publication (1993).
4. Psalm 94.8–11 (RSV translation).
5. Romans 1.20.
6. Cf. Tilby, op. cit., pp. 93–8.
7. William Wordsworth, 'A Slumber Did My Spirit Steal' in *Lyrical Ballads* (1789).
8. John Milton, *Paradise Lost*, X, ll. 668–71, 677–9, 711–12 etc.
9. The tsetse fly carries sleeping sickness. The symptoms include a 'drowsy lassitude preventing the victim from performing productive labour, or even vital acts of self-preservation'. So major a problem did it cause in some areas of central southern Africa that when Livingstone wrote his major book about Africa he put a portrait of this unamiable insect on the front cover – rather than a Bible.
10. Annie Dillard, *Pilgrim at Tinker Creek* (Picador, 1976), pp. 154–5.
11. Ibid., pp. 119, 121, 124.
12. Fred Hoyle, quoted in Paul Davies, *The Mind of God* (Simon & Schuster, 1992), p. 223.
13. Kenneth Clark.
14. Origen had originally been led to his typological (allegorical) reading of the Bible by discovering in the text patent nonsenses. He gives an example pointing to the Levitical instruction that people should not eat vultures: since, Origen claimed, no one could possibly want to eat a vulture there was

no point in forbidding it – and therefore there had to be a deeper meaning than at first appeared. Odd though this sounds to our ears, I would argue that it made more sense, in as much as it restored dignity to both God and the Bible reader, than the fossil-burying God of the nineteenth-century churchmen.

15. Teresa of Avila, *Book of Her Life*, ch. 22, section 8 in *Complete Works*, translated by E. Allison Peers, 1-vol. edn (Sheed & Ward, 1978), p. 139.

16. Hawking, op. cit., p. 140.

17. Jonathan Miller, quoted in Tilby, op. cit.

18. Hawking, op. cit., p. 174.

19. Davies, op. cit.

20. Keith Devlin, *Mathematics: The New Golden Age* (Pelican, 1988).

21. Tilby, op. cit., p. 9.

22. Sailors, in practice, had known this for a long time: navigation is impossible without a spherical geometry. Apparently they had spared mathematicians and philosophers this painful knowledge.

23. People who find this difficult to grasp should look at some of M. Escher's drawings where, using formally correct geometry, he creates on paper 'impossible' structures. Escher is an enormous help (and of course also a delight) when trying to visualize much of this material.

24. Bernard Shaw, quoted in J. Barrow, *Pi in the Sky* (Oxford University Press, 1993), p. 8.

25. Quoted in Devlin, op. cit., p. 129.

26. Interestingly, in India Jain philosophy had known this for a long time. Their logic admits a more sophisticated state of affairs. In Jainian descriptions of the truth or falsehood of a statement there are seven recognized positions: (1) maybe it is true; (2) maybe it is not; (3) maybe it is, but it is not; (4) maybe it is indeterminate; (5) maybe it is but is indeterminate; (6) maybe it is not but is indeterminate; (7) maybe it is and it is not and it is indeterminate. If you find these responses hard to get your head around perhaps you are too caught up in pre-quantum mind-sets! Alternatively, I have failed to outline them properly.

27. Douglas Hofstadter, *Metamagical Themas* (Basic Books, New York, 1985), p. 485.

28. John Barrow, quoted in Davies, op. cit.

29. These quotes are taken from Paul Davies, *The Mind of God*, which I have already commended to the interested reader. He develops this argument much more fully than I can do here. I need in fact to express a great debt to him for that book, other works, and his unusual accessibility and kindness in person.

30. Davies, op. cit., p. 61.

31. Sara Maitland, *Home Truths* (Chatto & Windus, 1993), p. 19.

32. Cf. Devlin, op. cit., p. 49.

33. Davies, op. cit., p. 231, partly quoting Rudy Rucker, *Infinity and the Mind* (Birkhauser, Boston, 1982), p. 48.

34. Bertrand Russell, *Mysticism and Logic* (1918).

35. G. H. Hardy, *A Mathematician's Apology* (1940), quoted in Devlin, op. cit., p. 75.

36. Gary Zukav, *The Dancing Wu Li Masters* (William Morrow, 1979), p. 93.

37. Dillard, op. cit., p. 134.

2   *What am I?*

I do not know how to write this chapter, I really do not know.

It seems strange, but the fact is that scientists, at the moment, know more about the most distant recesses of space and time than they know about what it is to be a human being. Some of this is a simple question of scale. There is a story about an astronomer opening a public lecture with a flourish: 'Basically', he announced, 'stars are quite dull.' A voice from the audience called out 'You'd look dull too from 25 light years away'. We might well find we knew less about stars than we think if we were able to see them close up. However the point remains: although we can describe the first few moments of the creation we cannot satisfactorily describe what makes us interested in the first few moments of creation. We do not have a working description of personality, of consciousness.

It is difficult to grasp and still more difficult to live with the enormous wild cosmos that I described in the previous chapter. We do not want a God of risk and chance. How many of us prefer, at least some of the time, a bossy nanny God who will order our every movement and keep us infantilized but safe? Despite the intellectual and emotional difficulties this kind of creation can be theologically acceptable to us. The Big Bang fits surprisingly easily into the structure of our older creation myth: 'God said, "Let there be light", and there was light.' God created the universe in a single radical act; a word spoken, a cosmic explosion, an ejaculation of power. Except for those people who need, for psychological reasons of their own, to read the Genesis account of creation as a scientific thesis instead of a poetic and theological narrative, the activities of God-out-there are not too threatening to our sense of self-esteem. But this security depends on us excluding ourselves from the large and alarmingly unregulated picture. We can accept indeterminacy, probability, complementarity and all those mind-boggling events and descriptions so long as we can believe that we, or at least our consciousness, are different – are unique, pure, special. We are observers of the show. We are just passing through. Matter is a temporary business; our true selves are spiritual. We don't really belong here, we belong in heaven – our true home – and therefore what goes on in this material universe is interesting but not important.

This is comforting, but untrue. Unfortunately it is no longer really possible to hold to this essentialist view of personhood. Or rather it is all too possible, but the price, including the denial of the evidence, is getting higher and higher. Paying that price requires of ordinary people a level of intellectual fraudulence. More unfortunately still, although the old view of the 'spiritual' soul locked into a material body is collapsing, it is not yet clear quite how to describe the situation that now appears to be the case. The problem of the self, of what it is to be a human individual, is proving somewhat intractable – both from the scientific and philosophic point of view.

I will try to put the problem simply. There is a perfectly common, normal feeling of integrity: I am the same person as I was when I was twenty, and when I was two. There is some continuity called me, Sara Maitland. To have no sense of this continuity is to be seriously ill. Yet it is undeniable that there is no material continuity or integrity – almost all the cells of my body have changed since then. Nor is there any clear intellectual continuity: I cannot think of a single idea in my head that I would articulate in the same way as I did 23 years ago. Even where I can at least partially observe the paths of change and development, there is something mysterious in the whole process. Obviously memory has something important to contribute to this debate, but this gives us a new set of questions: What is memory? How does it work? Where is it located? How can something so chancy and erratic as memory stabilize the whole of myself?

There are two general answers. There is the old dualist one: the 'real' self resides in the immortal soul, which takes up residence in a body for some purpose of God's and after it has finished with that body it will move on to the next thing, probably developed for good or bad but nonetheless essentially untouched by matter. Alternatively: the soul does not exist, materialism is all; our sense of there being something else simply demonstrates the sophistication of our neural hardware (or our genetic make-up, or our chemical flux). The trouble is that neither of these two descriptions is adequate. The 'story' of the self that they offer is not convincing; we need not only a better knowledge of the facts, but also a better myth, a more satisfying story.

The question of personhood, often called the mind/brain question, must now be the next major field of both scientific and philosophical inquiry. Already, pushed in part by biological advances in the understanding and mapping of our genetic inheritance and brain function on the one hand and by the capacity of computers to replicate intelligence on the other, new questions and new paradigms are being presented to us. AI – artificial intelligence – and virtual realities, quite apart from their delightful, provocative and speculative science fiction elements, undeniably force on us all questions about what it is to be a human person.

This brings me to Alan Turing, mathematical scientist, most famous for his wartime work on code breaking. He was part of the team which cracked the Enigma Code, the most important German secret communication method. Turing was also a remarkably original thinker. He is frequently credited with having invented the computer; he did not actually do so, but—just as Leonardo Da Vinci imagined a flying machine—Turing imagined, envisioned, how a universal computing machine would work. Turing was more fascinated by underlying questions than by technologies. One of the questions that he addressed was 'What does it mean to say that a machine "thinks"?' In 1950, in an article entitled 'Computing Machinery and Intelligence' he outlined a method for testing whether a machine could reasonably be said to think. This has become known as the Turing Test and is still broadly accepted as a working definition. In a Turing Test an observer cross-questions a machine and a reasonably intelligent human being, neither of which can be seen. The observers are not limited to asking computation questions but can and should range across the whole conversational landscape, including asking nonsense questions and emotional questions. Both the machine and the human being are 'programmed' to try and persuade the observer that they are the human being. If the observer consistently cannot distinguish between the person and machine, the machine is judged as 'thinking', and is deemed to have passed its Turing Test.

So far no machine has passed the Turing Test. However, many scientists believe this a technological problem rather than an ontological one. Such scientists believe that 'personhood' is the sum of the material parts. The brain, with its sophisticated neural network, is the place of personality and when we understand more how it works we will be able to make a computer that can do the same things. Other scientists however do not believe that any machine will ever pass a Turing Test. Roger Penrose,[1] the Cambridge physicist, for instance, argues that there is something going on in human beings that cannot be reduced to mechanics, even the most

71

advanced kinds; that human personality is more than its material parts. The brain is not all: there is something usually called mind which distinguishes human beings, and even animals, from the most advanced machine possible. He is not arguing that such a machine has not yet been made, but that one cannot be made because of the nature of mathematics and the nature of human beings.

As yet then there are no very satisfactory answers to this question. The responses offered by the various parties in this debate fail to satisfy. Neither the dualistic notions of the soul lodging temporarily in a body nor the pure scientific material-ism of the electronic wizards seem to describe what we experience as our selves.

This may be because of a profound arrogance: our desire to be special, to be the most important thing in the universe – indeed to have the universe made for us, for our benefit. Human pride is undoubtedly one of the most serious prob-lems the universe has to deal with, but a false humility, a denial of any subjectivity is no better. It is fair to test the scientific stories as we test the older theological and mythical stories. Frankly, the stories of the neuro-fundamentalists and other biological narrators are no better than the stories of the biblical fundamentalists. There is something absent from them which makes them not merely unsatisfactory but actually untrue.

Take a very tiny example: the neural circuits in our brains start to reverberate; chemical and electrical impulses, thus triggered, pass rapidly into our bodies. *Inter alia* they stimu-late the pituitary gland, which releases a sharp flow of hormones into the bloodstream. The body temperature rises half a degree on average, pulse and blood pressure increase, arteries and thoracic muscles contract, the vocal chords quiver, the lower jaw becomes suddenly uncontrollable and the spasms in lung and throat cause us suddenly to emit breath at approximately 70 miles an hour.

This is what happens when we laugh. It is a description of laughter, but it is not an explanation. It is not even an adequate account.

Many of the stories about the self offered by some geneticists and neurologists fall into the same category. We can accept their descriptions as 'correct' – certainly we should not be offering a definitive narrative that does not incorporate their descriptions fully and seriously – but we can still say that their explanations are inadequate; so inadequate that, although they may be correct, they are not true.

It seems to me that theology now has an opportunity to reclaim her ancient rôle as Queen of the sciences: that is, as the moderator and interpreter of these conflicting narratives. Theology, which has no particular axe to grind in this area, would seem to be well-placed to perform, for once, a useful rôle in a current intellectual debate. This is partly because the nature of the central claim of Christianity – that in Christ, God became fully human – has meant that the Christian community has spent a great deal of its intellectual energy over the last 2,000 years examining the question of what that humanity might be, what a normative humanity is. It is also because we, as Christians, have nothing to lose. We know, with a strange sort of confidence, that we draw our humanity from the God who created us. The more complex that humanity, that personhood, turns out to be, the more interesting our God becomes for us – the more marvellous and unpredictable. Even if the hardline brain-only materialists turn out to be right, and personality and individuality and all our feelings of passion and desire and love are 'just' the workings of our neural networks triggered by electrical impulses, we can stand confidently in the world our God has made, delighting in the brilliance of such an electrical engineer. Even if we can eventually make machines which do pass their Turing Test, and can think and feel just like human beings, we will have one more thing to thank God for – that we are made so intelligently and are allowed to participate so creatively in God's work. As in the strange world of subatomic particles and quantum thought, so here in the questions of the self, it is 'both our duty and our joy' to explore the parameters of personhood, with very little emotional investment in the result since *any* result will be to the glory of God.

However in order to deepen our joy and faith, and in order to be able to contribute to this debate within contemporary society at large, we will need to discipline ourselves. Much of the debate about the nature of the self is highly critical of Christian anthropology and philosophy. In particular, many secular intellectuals are fiercely opposed to Christian Neoplatonism and to the various dualistic or over-spiritualized models of personhood that have been on offer. Much Christian thinking on this issue has been crudely consolatory or tediously abstract. We need to take up a stance which is neither defensive nor aggressive, but genuinely open-minded. We need to practise what can perhaps best be described as a radical orthodoxy: this is, to hold firm to the deposit of truth, and hold as light as possible to the expression of it.

I am always surprised, to be honest, when I am accused of being theologically radical. This usually comes the other way round: people are surprised by my failure to be as radical as they expected. 'How could a radical like you become a Roman Catholic?' I have been asked so many times in the last year. When I reply I never was a radical, people tend to feel cheated. I think of myself, and always have since my conversion to Christianity nearly a quarter of a century ago, as deeply orthodox in the catholic tradition. Unless the mere thought of a lay woman thinking, writing and talking theologically is *per se* 'radical', I cannot think of anything I have ever said or done to make anyone think otherwise. If this is the case, it is a very new error given that Mary Magdalen was the first person we know of charged with proclaiming the resurrection. I have never found the deposit of faith deficient at the metaphysical level. Where I do have difficulties is in the ethical and practical working out of that deposit. This is nearly always because I find many of these workings-out unorthodox: they do not flow from traditional 'sound doctrine'.

Take, for example, the vexed question of appropriate pronouns for God. Traditional, orthodox doctrine, for once arm in arm with common sense, teaches us that God is without qualities. Gender is, by any definition, a 'quality' in the classical sense: therefore God doesn't have it. Gender is also a feature of *biology* and God doesn't have any of that either, I might add. The only ways you can express gender-free personhood in contemporary English are by (1) eliminating all pronouns altogether – this is perfectly possible, but grammatically very hard work; or (2) by constantly – in all sentences – saying both, which is both tedious and ugly; or (3) by playing with the concepts. As a matter of fact I have never met a *Christian* feminist who wants to deny the Fatherhood of God; only those who want to extend our range of images and metaphors in the joyful but constantly doomed struggle to measure up to our Big-Enough God. Indeed one cannot help but wonder what is going on in the mind of someone who objects to female (that is, personalist) language for God, but does not protest about descriptions of the Second Person of the Trinity as a fruit-bearing plant (the vine) or a geological formation (a rock), to use more ancient and authoritative instances. I proudly claim both orthodoxy and tradition here, over those who wish to assign to God biological qualities.

Anyway this apparent diversion in defence of my own theological orthodoxy is really because I am proposing that, in the struggle to understand personhood in the light of the contemporary state-of-the-art sciences, the fundamental expressions of rigid orthodoxy are helpful. Christianity has two particularly helpful ideas here, and with peculiar perversity they are two that modern liberal theology apparently most wants to dispose of: the forgiveness of sins and the resurrection of the body. I believe that if the Church could take on board a proper, theologically thought-out understanding of what scientists and sociologists have 'discovered' about the human condition in the last hundred years, we wouldn't have this bashful embarrassment about these two most useful and profound articles of our faith. Moreover in the light of such a theology we would be able not merely to nourish our own hope and faith, but also help those who are beleaguered by biologism and desperately seeking a wider, more convincing, story of their own selves.

In the previous chapter I wrote at length about how the mathematical and physical sciences were offering us a new view of how the cosmos – the created order at large – might be perceived: not as a clockwork toy wound up by a technician God, but as a living art work, with risk and creativity built in, laid on, inherent to the project. Far from the deity being forced into a limited rôle as *primum mobile* (like the Princess of Wales switching on the Oxford Street Christmas lights to open up an orgy of materialism) or being reduced to a God-of-the-Gaps, slowly reasoned out of existence as the frontiers of science are rolled back; God is present in that dynamic process of chance, throwing dice with delight so to speak. God is not the ghost in the machine, as a nineteenth-century scientist put it, 'not because there is no ghost but because there is no machine'.[2]

Now I want to take this idea a stage further. What the so-called hard sciences have done for the cosmos, the soft sciences – both the life sciences (biology and chemistry) and the social sciences (psychology, sociology, geography and so forth) – have done for the human sense of identity. As I said at the beginning of this chapter, in one way this is more frightening.

In another sense it is easier. We have to take on trust the data that the astrological and the subatomic scientists offer us.

I cannot do the maths and I have no access to radio telescopes nor particle accelerators. Moveover the data that they provide us with imply a reality which is in total contradiction to that common sense, against which I, like most people, was brought up to test proposals. I do in fact believe what the scientists are telling us – mainly because I cannot imagine what interest they would have in a vast collective conspiracy to lie to me; and because they monitor each other so strictly. When it comes to the human sciences it is in one sense much easier to check out the scientists. We ourselves are the data, the experimental material and the objects to be investigated. There is therefore a direct way in which I can inspect and test the conclusions that they come to. Does this make sense? Does this satisfy? Does this accord with my own experience of myself?

At the beginning of her immensely amusing and helpful book *The Descent of Woman*,[3] Elaine Morgan challenged the then fashionable evolutionists who argued human behaviour from animal origins, like Ardrey and Morris. Among other things she urged her readers to apply their sweeping generalizations to specific examples. 'Man is the most sophisticated predator known to the universe, who uses killing as the primary way of settling disputes' has a magnificent and persuasive ring to it. However it sounds totally different when you apply it – 'My grocer is the most sophisticated predator known to the universe'; 'My child's primary teacher uses killing as her primary way of settling disputes.' Morgan suggested fairly convincingly that there was a great deal of (male) wish-fulfilment going on in such books: people liked the idea of themselves as ferocious predators, driven by needs deeper and more authentic than the need to co-operate. Her underlying point – that one can test ideas or claims about the self against the primary example of one's own self – remains valid, whatever those claims may be. Of course, we too may indulge ourselves in fantasy and be unwilling to look clearly at the facts – and those of us who believe in God will naturally be accused of just this by more determined materialists. This works in reverse too – I catch myself wondering what pride or infantile arrogance so limits the vision of rigidly materialist thinkers. Nonetheless in looking at personhood there is a real way in which what is claimed must correspond somewhere, at some level, to what is our own sense of ourselves.

Despite this, I admit to finding it hard to grasp really and finally that, if there is a show going on, we are not the audience. We cannot be the audience, and there is no place 'outside' where we can take a seat and settle down to watch. The risky and changing nature of the universe, its slow history and its internal creativity, goes on in me, in us all, as much as in the furthest star. Indeed the two are not so separate or different, for the stuff of which I am made and the far-flung stars are made is the same stuff.

One question worth asking is *why* it should feel so difficult to accept the idea that we are dumped on the stage, part of the show, 'our bones the bones of the old red stars',[4] animated star dust in the process of becoming something else. Why do we instinctively prefer the idea that we are outside the rest of the world of matter, superior to it, dominating and controlling it? Why do we need to believe that the whole thing is somehow all laid on for our express benefit? Why are we apparently able to accept a more random view of the world order so long as we are exempted from it? Let the scientists have their fun; we don't mind and nor does God, but do not let them touch our own anthropocentricity.

'God made the universe in seven days' or 'In the beginning there was a Big Bang . . . ' It does not really matter which; either will do because we still hang on to the second half of the mediaeval world-view: that it was all made, by whatever means, for ME. Humanity is the end and purpose of the whole thing. All the world is a stage, and we are the audience.

This leads to certain quite particular, and rather dangerous, conceits. For example, just as the world was made to be nurse and mother to God's favourite offspring; so Man, like God, could lay his seed – made in his image, the complete little child – in the womb of a mother, where it would be nurtured, protected and grown to fullness. Although most people have abandoned this particular biological model, many do not seem to be able to give up the psychological egocentrism that the biology allowed. Male human beings still often seem to act as though they were gods, and as though women were the field of their labours.

Of course it is hard to give it up, this comforting model. One of the reasons it is hard is that we still cling tenaciously to a profound dualism which neither theology nor any of the other sciences seems able to extirpate.

The attempt to express the central mystery of the Incarnation which is 'folly to the Jews and a scandal to the Greeks', in formal terms acceptable to both, has left us with a dualistic heritage which is both hidden and irradicable. It keeps turning up to haunt us. We want to say that Jesus is fully human and fully God without saying he is sort of bits of each. However the language of classical philosophy simply cannot express it. An eternal, immutable, necessary God and a contingent, transient, mortal human being: this is a two-into-one-won't-go situation. The early Church 'saw off' Christological heresy after Christological heresy – Arianism, Nestorianism, Docetism, Adoptianism, and many others – in an attempt to get this equation right. Yet even the elaborations of the Athanasian Creed sound weak and floundering when they come to Christology.

> Furthermore it is necessary to everlasting salvation that he also believe rightly in the Incarnation of Our Lord Jesus Christ. For the right faith is that we believe and confess that Our Lord Jesus Christ, the Son of God, is God and man. God of the substance of the Father, begotten before all worlds, and Man of the substance of

his mother, born in the world. Perfect God and perfect
Man of a reasonable soul and human flesh subsisting.
Equal to the Father as touching his Godhead and
inferior to the Father as touching his Manhood. Who
although he be God and Man, yet he is not two but one
Christ.[5]

As though all this was not complicated and tricky enough in
itself, at the same time the early Christian intellectuals were
wrestling with another set of heresies which were dualist in a
more absolute sense – they were anti matter, anti the body.
Manichaeism and Gnosticism in all its forms argued that
matter was Bad, was negative in itself. Spirit, manifested in the
pure immortal soul was Good, was real, was perfect, but – woe
and alas – it had got stuck inside these tiresome, disagreeable,
malevolent things called bodies, which were – to mis-context a
quotation – 'mean, nasty, brutish and short'.

This idea of the person coming in two bits as it were, the
soul (good) and the body (bad), is deeply embedded in our
thought and language patterns, in our self-understanding
and in our identity. The dangers of such dualistic thinking
have been, of late, repeatedly pointed out, particularly though
not exclusively by feminist theologians, who link the injustices
against and diminishment of women closely to dualistic mind-
sets: the pattern of God, men and soul on one side and nature,
women and body on the other, and the assumed superiority of
the former.[6] This insistence on a return to a more proper and
orthodox unitive model, which is necessary to make any sense
of the Incarnation as a theological event, is perhaps one of the
most important contributions that feminist theology has
made.

There has, however, turned out to be an unexpected
problem with this body of feminist theology, especially from
the USA. Having diagnosed and attempted to cure the
dualistic disease it promptly contracted another form of it – by

taking an idealist, or essentialist, view of 'experience' which deftly replaced the concept of 'the soul', while something called 'conditioning' replaced the concept of the body. 'Experience' now is Good – pure, true, real – while 'conditioning' is always Bad – 'false', temporary, imposed. It afflicts the pure self from outside. Experience, in feminist theology, now functions exactly as the soul did in the theologies that are being criticized.

This is not an easy idea to understand, but it is an important one, I think. The error is certainly not confined to feminist theologians although it is rather clearly expressed in our work.

> What is necessary is a critical appraisal of the notion of 'women's experience' which plays a central rôle in these forms of theology and spirituality. There is a discernible tendency to use experience as an essentialist notion – that is, to imply that deep down in every woman, under all the layers of false conditioning there is a pure nugget of unique personal experience: the function of 'true religion' or 'feminism' or whatever is then to reveal this new self in all its pristine glory. It is an attitude which refuses in the last analysis to see experience as that which is constructed in ideology and therefore falls into the ideological trap.[7]

Watch it! West is saying here, even feminists are not immune to the evil virus of dualism. If you buy even a small chunk of this sort of essentialist thinking there are consequences. One of the consequences is that you will not be able to tell the truth. Frankly, the idea of the pure, additive-free, suitable for vegans, proven 'soul' or 'experience' or 'consciousness' that exists outside the time—space—matter continuum is heretical, and wrong-headed. The idea that 'something' comes to lodge or be imprisoned in that temporary cage called the body or history or society, which it will later shuck off and dispose of, and that this uneasy and inherently unstable amalgam is what it is to be a human person, a self, is dualist. It is also not what the evidence from the social sciences bears witness to. It may be like that for angels, for extra-terrestrials and for the characters of late bourgeois fiction, but it is not so for us.

Regrettably or otherwise, what it is to be a person is to have a body and everything that goes with that. To have a body is to have also a gender, a class, a time, a history, an education, a psychology, a cultural location, a genetic inheritance and a bit of blind luck. It is to have all those things that are traditionally called 'qualities', precisely the things that we are taught that God does not have. This is why the 'made in her image' language is so difficult. If there are no images of God, how can we be made in them?

We do not know how God's personhood exists, although we live in the hope and faith that it does exist. Meanwhile for ourselves we have to acknowledge that personhood is constructed out of all these messy material things. Personhood isn't a given, an eternal flash of genius from the mind of the maker. It is the consequence of a long hard haul: out of the Big Bang; in from the coagulating cosmic dust; up from the hot seas 500 million years ago; down from the trees on the edge of the grassy plain; out through the vagina of the women who bore us; across the treacherous terrains of childhood; into consciousness. We cannot do it alone either; so much of the work of making us was done before we were even thought of. A chic word in social and ecclesial theology at the moment is *koinonia*: what it *is* to be a person is to be an individual-in-community; just as what it is to be a biological organ is to be in a body within an interplay of organs, a unit of a whole. What it is to be a meaningful word is to be part of a sentence; what it is to be a number is to be part of a coherent sequence. None of these images denies the integrity of the individual unit, they just put it in its place.

So it is with the self. Rowan Williams in his book *Resurrection* puts it thus:

> The self at any given moment is a made self – it is not a solid independent machine for deciding and acting efficiently or rationally in response to stimuli, but is itself a process, fluid and elusive, whose present range of possible responses is part of a developing story. The self *is* – one might say – what the past is doing now. It is continuity and so it is necessarily memory – continuity seen as the shape of a unique story, my story, which I own, acknowledge as mine. To be a self is to own such a story; to act as a self is to act out of the awareness of this resource of a particular past.[8]

In the abundance and ebullience of God's creative energy we co-create our own personhood. What perhaps this snippet from Williams's profound (and beautiful) meditation on the self does not quite make clear is how communal, how social this process necessarily is. We co-create ourselves in community. We co-create ourselves in community with the astral bodies that lie beyond the space horizon; and we co-create ourselves in community with our neighbours. It is all these communities that also, simultaneously, co-create the parameters within which this construction of personhood, this making of the self, can happen. This is the 'cosmic dance', and you *cannot* 'tell the dancer from the dance'.[9]

This co-creation is chancy, risky, random even, and too often doomed, but it is not lawless. The laws that govern the chancy, random behaviour of matter at the subatomic level, which I discussed in the previous chapter, have been discovered only in the last century or so. The same is true of the laws which we currently believe to govern, or control, this chancy random construction of the self. I believe that in fact the two cannot be separated.

These new scientific rules, these parameters, are complex – and the relationships between them are still more complex. However we are supposed to enjoy complexity and intricacy and paradoxical relationships, so do not be afraid.

I am no more an expert in the social sciences than I am in the physical sciences or the theological sciences: as I said at the very beginning I am an amateur – a lover – and a lay person. Nonetheless I am, boldly, going to give you a short guided tour of a few of the 'laws' which govern the co-creative construction of human personhood. I should perhaps add at this point that, on the same terms, we cannot set up any of the 'laws' I am about to outline as absolutes, as gods in the older sense. They too exist as parts, fluid parts, of the whole. I would like, without diverting to study this in any detail, to point out

> Raymond Williams' argument that social structures are constantly in the process of constitution. Structures identified by analysis such as ideology, language, power, the State, the relations of production, sexuality and so forth exist only in solution, they are not absolutely prior to the subject [the self] but themselves always in the process of formation.[10]

This is too often forgotten, I feel, by many scientists, who seem to want to believe that *their* discourse, unlike anyone else's, is objective. Their own methodologies are free, untainted by the subjectivity of the observer and existing completely independently. I suggested in the previous chapter that mathematics, because of its subject matter, might be able to make this claim, but the life sciences most certainly cannot – less so now than ever.

Nonetheless, with all these caveats in place, I would like, briefly, to look at a list of more or less contemporary ideas which over the last two centuries have undermined the essentialist understanding of the human soul as pre-existent and immutable.

(1) *Evolution*   When Darwin published his *The Origin of Species* in 1859, he achieved a rare accolade: the profound importance of a work of ideas was recognized immediately. The book sold out before publication. It created an intellectual ferment that is hard to understand now. From pulpits to cartoons in *Punch* the responses were immediate and impassioned. The controversy that the book generated was instant and violent: we live still in the ripples of that impact. *The Origin of Species* enshrined not so much a brand new idea, but an explanation of, a plausible mechanism for a concept that was already hovering in the wings.

In the decades before *The Origin of Species* was published there had been a steady undermining of confidence in the Genesis account of creation. The increased numbers of, and the desire to understand, fossil remains; the researches of historians and anthropologists and particularly archaeologists; the sense of being at home in a world so much larger than that of the biblical or classical societies; the rapid industrialization and urbanization of Western society; and other factors, had already threatened the literal interpretation of the biblical narratives. By the middle of the nineteenth century many people were prepared for the notion that the Genesis stories of the creation and the flood were not a fully adequate account of the earliest history of humanity or even the planet. Contrary to what I was taught in primary school, by 1859 lots of people already knew that we were not simply plonked down in Eden ready-made, except for sartorial taste. Jean Baptiste de Lamarck, for example, had already proposed a model for evolution. He believed in the inheritance of learned characteristics, so that skills learned by experience in one generation were handed down to the next; so that a giraffe that had stretched its neck reaching up for higher leaves would pass a longer neck on to its offspring. Lamarck also wrote about evolution by desire: that a species striving for a higher form of life could develop one.

The shock impact of *The Origin of Species* came not from the idea that life forms evolved, but from the demonstration of how this could happen randomly, through mutation. Not merely was *Homo sapiens* descended from monkeys – to put it a great deal too crudely – but they had so developed by chance, by random mutation and aggressive adaptation: neither directed nor ethical. This seemed, to worthy Victorian theologians, bizarrely too risky for the sort of God they were expecting to find: a God of Newtonian physics and imperial expansion. The social application of Darwinism was surprisingly quickly evident to conservative theologians. It did not sit easily with cheerful beliefs like:

> The rich man in his castle,
> The poor man at his gate;
> God made them high and lowly
> And ordered their estate.

(a verse which has mercifully been removed from most contemporary hymn books, even if not from the subconsciouses of too many contemporary Christians).

Despite a desperate rearguard action – which began among educated divines and is still continued by some biblical fundamentalists – Darwinian evolution won swift acceptance and consent. It has proved an immensely successful scientific theory: it has broad applicability and excellent predictive powers. It also appears to strike satisfying emotional chords; even the Church has managed to come to terms with it.

The basic concepts of Darwinism have hardly been challenged since. The only problem with the theory was how the mechanism of mutation might work. Darwin was himself aware of this flaw and did not know what to do about it. The discovery of DNA a century later answered the problem.

DNA and the genetic sciences confirmed Darwinism. It demonstrated that genes were the necessary 'something' to do the mutating, and that the genetic code was laid down at the moment of conception.[11]

Since the discovery of the double helix and how it transmits qualities from one generation to the next, our understanding of inheritance has grown very fast. A great number of human characteristics are now believed to have a genetic origin. Recently it has become possible to envisage a time when every part of the gene will be understood (we will know what each tiny bit is *for*). A worldwide research project, called the Human Genome Map, has been initiated to track down the details of the genetic code. This international co-operation has caused a widespread deep ethical concern, but little sense of adventurous excitement. Although the concern is real and necessary, particularly as it becomes increasingly possible to test the genetic make-up and alter the genetic code of unborn children, we should also recognize the extraordinary knowledge about ourselves that this project will give us. It will inevitably lay open the way that our personhood is structured in the couplings that lead to our conceptions. The interest aroused by the very small-scale and somewhat dubious research published in 1993, which suggested that there was a genetic predisposition to male homosexual behaviour, was also accompanied by wild speculation about what evolutionary advantage this could give individuals or social groups. The idea that genes are 'the answer' to questions about our humanity and individuality has grown into our consciousness extremely quickly.

Thus evolution, and within it biological inheritance, provides the first parameter in the process of self-creation – not just at the macro level, but at the, so to speak, domestic level as well. We carry this deep 'memory' in our cells, and we carry too the genetic inheritance within the species. It should also be remembered that our personhood is structured by the personal habits of our parents and the care, or otherwise, we all take of our environment. Radioactive irradiation, for example, is now known to affect the DNA, causing mutations which can change what sort of person a yet unborn human being will be.

The acceptance of evolution, of genetic mutation and inherited characteristics, is so general that we often fail to notice how much it undercuts ideas of autonomy and independence, and therefore how profoundly it ties us to each other and to the whole of cosmic history. I am who I am because of the ecological and other circumstances that randomly happened to be going on, not just at one magical moment called 'creation', but over and over and over again throughout the period that there has been organic life on this planet. We are not just talking about the colour of our eyes or the length of our legs. There are close connections between physical and mental characteristics. It is not just that certain personality traits are probably genetic in origin and therefore inherited. We are rapidly becoming aware that the sort of body and brain that you are born with affect the development of those characteristics which are learned rather than inherited. The human person, we are learning somewhat uncomfortably, simply does not exist outside the chancy entwinings of the double helix.

(2) *Class* Less than a decade after Darwin had shown us how the long slow making of our contemporary selfhood was worked on by the blind mating habits of therapsids, Marx published the first volume of *Das Kapital* and showed us another facet, another dimension of the process of the co-creating of persons. Economics, hard materialism – 'class' he called it – did not just make people rich or poor, it made people.

It is interesting that while Darwinism very rapidly became acceptable, Marxist theory never has. This would seem to be because it superficially carries with it a great deal of moral baggage, although Marx himself did not mean it to – which is why it was called scientific socialism. Unlike the utopian or idealistic socialisms that preceded it, Marxism offered not a project for the future but an analysis of the present – more like the prophets of the Scriptures than like the Delphic Sibyl. Capitalism *would* fall into terminal crisis and from that crisis *would* evolve either the socialist revolution or what Marx called barbarism. As it happens capitalism has proved much more resilient than Marx allowed for – for one thing international capitalism has recognized its shared interests, and limited the amount and extent of market competition between nations. Nonetheless Marx's claim that economics is the base – the fundamental determinate of who we as individuals are – and that everything else is secondary superstructure, remains deeply persuasive. Everyone's 'experience' of life, and therefore their consciousness of self and other, is radically affected by their relation to the means of production. So profoundly are we created within this particular system that it is hard to see how it works in practice, beyond the crudest levels. For instance, if one is born in one set of economic circumstances one will probably be dead before one has a chance to achieve consciousness at all!

The conspicuous failure of political structures to deliver a cure for this disease of class, far from negating Marx's point about personhood, actually underlines it. The apparently intractable boundaries that history and the individual's economic and class location within it imposes on personality have been accepted, for instance, by liberal relativism in relation to ethics and judgement, even where no open credence would be given to Marxist ideology. The whole thrust of liberation theology, and indeed large parts of all Christian struggle for justice, is motivated by the belief that personhood is distorted, is affected and altered by economic and other material realities.

Dialectic materialism and Christianity have declared war on each other, but this may be a mistaken enterprise. In

Chapter 1 I noted that the two ideologies both viewed time with a real seriousness: in that context 'time' was an enormous and abstract concept. Here it is a much smaller and more precise one: both view *history* with a real seriousness, with a real commitment to discerning the signs of the times and acknowledging 'the fullness of time'.

In Greek there are two different words to express two different senses in which we use the single word 'time'. *Chronos* means the measured passing of the minutes, time as a fixed and regular event: as in chronology, chronicle. *Kairos* means time in the sense of a significant moment. Marxism and Christianity share a sense of *kairos*, a belief that what can and should happen at one moment in chronological time cannot (or should not) happen at another, because the circumstances of the time, of the historical particularity, are part of what create the possibility. The mediaeval world-view, the perceptions of the apostolic age, the time of the apocalypse are all discrete because they are made moments: they are constructed by events created by made persons, made selves, in whom history, time, class and relationships have been at work. They are not transferable.

Self is a product of history and class relationships and economics, which are all themselves constructions of past or present selves. There is reciprocity and creativity but no absolute freedom. Battered and discredited though Marxist ideas may be, the boundaries of freedom and autonomy that Marx laid down do seem to hold.

(3) **Gender** I am cooking the books a little to enter gender here. Moreover I can hear the 'what about race?' question being raised already, and rightly so. Nonetheless I am going to talk about gender for a number of reasons, some of which I will quickly try to explain.

(a) It is how I got to think about all these issues in the first place. The demands that the women's liberation movement made of me in the early 1970s, just as I became an adult, were of such force and such intoxicating delight that they triggered in me an interest in all the ideas that I am writing about in this book, including God.

(b)   It is in the light of my relation to questions of gender that I get to publish this book at all. Feminism has allowed and encouraged those women who have engaged with it to transgress across the traditional boundaries of intellectual disciplines – it has authorized amateurs to speak. If I am a theologian at all I am a 'feminist theologian'. In one sense I believe this to be a false category – since any theology that is not related to justice and truth is not theological, and any truth claim that leaves out 52 per cent of the people in the world is really most unlikely to be very competent. Nonetheless I am a feminist before I am a theologian: feminism is what I do and what I am known for doing.

(c)   The period of time which I am looking at in this list of ideas which have dethroned the idea of an eternal, stable and fixed self – the Western nineteenth and twentieth centuries – is so precisely the period of the women's movement that it is impossible not to see some connection. I think there is a very close connection. A central intellectual claim of the women's movement is that things do not have to be as things always have been; that femininity, for example, is not 'natural' in the sense of immutable or transcendent, but is socially constructed. More, feminism has argued consistently that the social construction of gender changes both in time and in place; and that it can be deconstructed (a process most popularly known as revolution, but within Christianity more comfortably called transformation). This reflects so limpidly the claims of post-Einsteinian physics (that the position of the observer affects the phenomenon observed), of evolutionary theory (that things are not now as they always were), and of theories of class (that the social and economic circumstances affect personhood) that it would be preposterous not at least to note the coincidence.

(d) The Christian Church has proved stubbornly resistant to recognizing the significance of gender in the construction of the subject self. Most official theology clings to a preposterous self-contradiction. The immortal soul, being as it were a spark of the divine, is without gender, as God is; but God must always be grammar-ed (if such a participle exists) as male, and discrimination against souls which happen to be lurking about in female bodies is not only legitimate, but is the will of God. It does not seem too difficult to see that this is at best incoherent, and rather more probably nonsensical.

I do not for one moment want to acquit the religiously powerful of the charges of racism and class bias. However at the theoretical level at least Christianity has taught that in God's eyes black and white people; rich and poor people; capitalists, artisans, intelligentsia, the proletariat and the lumpenproletariat are equal. There may even, it is tentatively argued, be an actual bias towards the oppressed in God's plan. When it comes to gender, however, the Church has never spoken clearly and has always justified discrimination on theological grounds. In one sense this is lucky because it leaves open a chink in the armour of the nonsensical idea that the body has nothing to do with the real core of a human being. Christian theology since the Pauline writings – that is, for as long as we have any record of its content – has stumbled over gender, and in that stumbling revealed at the very centre a deep confusion about what it is to be a human person.

(e) Gender itself, as a biological phenomenon, is not dilutable or even dispensable. That difference is immutable. The interpretation of its meaning is of course transformable and has been transformed repeatedly, but the actual solid fact that human beings come in one of two kinds – male or female – is simply a given of the species. It is possible to imagine that there could be a society in which class differences had ceased to exist; or in which social development had so mixed the genetic pool that racial origin was no longer traceable. It is not possible to imagine a society in which maleness and female-ness had been bred out or socially eliminated. In this sense gender is a creator of personhood which stands outside of historical development – it is a difference that is as elementary as life itself. It demonstrates that the differences between human beings, the sorts of persons that we can be, really are determined, at least in part, by our very existence. Race or class may be a consequence of sin; they may not exist in God's original scheme, in God's perfect will. Gender is not like that: it is an absolute necessary human condition, a *sine qua non*.

It would be nice to think that this apologetic diversion has been unnecessary.

However, to return to the matter at hand: Almost all sociological studies suggest that gender is a fixed parameter in the development of personhood. The 'nature' versus 'nurture' debate continues unabated, but the differences between female human beings and male human beings are *there*. It does not matter here what meaning one ascribes to those differences.[12] What does matter is that the sort of person one is is fundamentally affected by which of the two sorts of available bodies one happens to be. Virginia Woolf and many of her contemporaries who held on to ideas of a dream-place androgyny were denying a reality in which they experienced that difference. The element of wishful thinking is painfully clear in a simultaneous reading of *Orlando* and *A Room of One's Own* or *Three Guineas*.

The slow discovery of how much difference gender makes is in a sense the history of the women's movement. Mary Wollstonecraft argued in her *Vindication of the Rights of Women* that with equality of education alone the differences between the genders would evaporate. She has been disproved. We have learned how deep the difference goes. Some feminists now believe that women are simply a superior sort of human being – innately predisposed towards peace, unitive succour-ing and green good sense. (It is perhaps fair to mention here that I myself incline to a more-nurture-than-nature position and am unable, in my more honest moments, to believe myself less capable of sin than my male neighbour.) However they understood the difference, feminists and their opponents have never questioned that gender constructed the person; that the self was unquestionably formed within biological and social frameworks which were not androgynous and not identical.

This idea of radical and unchangeable difference emerged in the nineteenth century mainly because it had not forced itself as a question before then. It is interesting for example that there does not seem to have been any theological discussion about why Jesus was a male human being rather than a female human being before the nineteenth century. The matter was not discussed because it does not seem to have occurred to anyone to question the 'obvious' choice of representative humanity being male. The realization of how profoundly self is created within the definitions of gender is a modern understanding. It is one that could only have arisen, I suspect, within the social context of the post-Enlightenment and ideas of inalienable and 'self-evident' 'human rights'. The newness of the idea however does nothing to make it more or less true; the idea that gender is somehow new *and therefore trivial* is as absurd as the idea that evolution is insignificant because it was not discovered in the prehistorical era.

(4) *Psychoanalysis* Having put in place these three de-stabilizers of the 'pure-soul' – the whole person formed in heaven by God, draped in a rather trendy outfit called the body and shrunk small enough to fit into a uterus – the nineteenth century clearly felt that it had done its bit. Freud did not publish *The Interpretation of Dreams* until 1900. For any dualistic view of human personhood psychoanalytical theory is the One Big One. Christian theology still has not entered into any sort of relationship with psychoanalytical theory,

although it uses – often appallingly badly – psychotherapeutic techniques and jargons.

Interestingly, theology's attitudes towards a great deal of post-Freudian work closely resembles its attitudes towards Galileo 250 years earlier – 'Try and shut him up, and if that fails ignore the whole thing'. Now this is not really surprising because there are real and close parallels between the theological import of both men's work. They both dethrone the supposed 'special relationship' between God and Man (and I use this latter word advisedly).

Galileo made impossible the view of ourselves as the centre, the purpose and the climax of the universe; where we can stand at peace in a small still place – perfect, eternal, immutable, designer-made for our convenience – and all the planets, all the great powers, dance around us and their dance is edifying and delightful. Wrong, said Galileo: *Eppur si muove*, he said, it *does* move. Forced, eventually, to abandon its anthropocentric universe, Christianity privatized itself, but it never changed the model. Now inside each *individual* was a small, still place – perfect, eternal, immutable, designer-made – called the self or the soul, and around it the body danced for its edification though rather less, alas, for its delight (astral bodies being less into sex than human bodies they were more permitted to be delightful). The image is more of a gym training session for the soul: if, without getting too involved, too moved, the soul could get the body to behave well it could move on, unchanged, to higher things.

Then Freud said the equivalent of *Eppur si muove*. He said personhood is forged in the act of living; self grows and develops through experience – and worse still through forgetting experience, or through reconverting experience. He insisted that a person is not a machine that can be made to behave by the soul programming the body to 'act virtuously'. He made clear that the movements of the subconscious are as real as the acts of the conscious, of the will. Just as Galileo offered a mechanism to explain the celestial phenomena, Freud offered a mechanism to explain Paul's tragic lament against the plight of the human condition: 'That which I would I do not; and I do even that which I would not.'

Some of Freud's specific theories have been disproven and abandoned, but the impact that psychoanalysis has had on our understanding of personhood is extraordinary. It affects us at every level—in cultural production, and language and theories of education. From his basic ideas spring coils of complexity and intricacy and co-responsibility; opening whole areas of human life to new understanding and new expression. Childhood for instance, and with it the duties of parents and education, is changed for ever: innocence is banished, but potential is increased. It is still hard to integrate this knowledge with the older one: the virulence of the public response when young children are convicted of violent crimes shows how little we desire an adult view. In good sense it should be less horrible that ten-year-olds should kill than that adults should: traditionally the business of growing up is the business of learning control. However the mean violence of outraged sensibility spoke to our deep desire to keep children innocent, of our weakness in the face of this threat to our peace of mind, despite nearly a hundred years of knowing 'better'.

No one is arguing that it is more comfortable to accept corporate, social responsibility for the personhood, the self, of each individual within the community. I joke that I abandoned Freud the day my first child was born. As long as I was only a daughter the idea that it was 'all the mother's fault' was extremely attractive. The day I became a mother the idea seemed intolerable and painful. It is of course, much cosier, much easier to dump all the blame on God; but God, it seems to me, revealed in the way the world actually is (as opposed to the dualistic way we would like it to be), goes on patiently handing the responsibility back to us. God calls on us to be grown-ups, and fellow workers, offering us a difficult but exciting task – creating one another's humanity. Freud speaks to this understanding: the language we use, the bodies we have and the ways we act, especially towards children but continuously towards each other, is mutually self-creating. It matters what we do. Persons, selves, are continually coming into becoming in our every act. It is a responsibility too big to be endured were it not for the fact of that co-creation being shared by God, and potentially absolved in the passion of Christ.

There is one note of caution I would like to strike here. There is a danger that if we take the idea of a 'processed self' too simplisticly we may deny selfhood to those who are disabled from process – the very young child, the severely brain-damaged or the comatose, for example. The dangers of dehumanizing, depersonalizing any group of human beings must stand as part of the 'common sense' that I suggested at the beginning of this chapter we could use to monitor theories of the self. If this idea of the co-creation of human persons ends by depersonalizing anyone then the idea itself must be fundamentally wrong. However, I think this concept of the made self, constructed personhood, only endangers the already marginalized when it is understood too simplisticly. If this process of co-creation is understood truly corporately, as it should be, things become more complicated but more hopeful. For just as the mother creates the child's self, the child creates the mother; a woman is not, cannot be, mother without the child. Of course she does not become mother to the obliteration of other personae and characteristics, but there is no such thing as being abstractly 'mother': mother is the experience of mothering a particular person. Thus by its very existence the child creates, with the mother, an aspect of who the mother is, the mother's self.[13]

The same is true of all relationships, even reluctant or refusing ones: a 'carer' like a lover exists because they care for someone; a murderer comes into being by murdering somebody. The person in need of care, the object of the murderer's lethal activities are co-creating that particular and differentiated self. Therefore it seems impossible to be so far outside the human community that one does not participate in the work of the co-creation of selves, of self. Simply what it is to have personhood, to be a self, is not only to act but to be acted upon. This is not passive, in the traditionally understood sense, because to be acted upon by another *is* to act upon that other – by the nature of our humanity, by the nature of our *koinonia*.

As we move into the twentieth century, the list of parameters within which we do co-create personhood expands into a multiplicity of disciplines – psycholinguistics, for instance, and semiotics, both of which suggest once again but particularly strongly that identity does *not* come as a given lump but is made by and within culture. Some newer theories of the imagination, particularly ideas about the *Zeitgeist* and the collective unconscious, elaborate the ways in which past selves participate in the making of new selves. There are whole areas of sociology and even geography and topography that reveal the same message. 'Alone with none but thee my God / I journey on my way' is simply not true – there is no 'I' alone. We are bound to each other not just as an ethical prescription, but as a fact of our existence.

This is not a recipe either for chaos or for determinism. It is not chaotic because all these things are available for inspection, criticism and analysis. Just as the laws of physics really do produce meaningful predictions so the 'laws' of human-ness, of personhood, do the same, at least in the quantum sense of offering probabilities. It is not deterministic because intricacy and creativity are genuinely built in. I am not saying that it is too complicated for us to be able to predict what sort of self we will create by what sort of acts: this would be merely a version of the God-of-the-Gaps for the social sciences. I am saying that the randomness – and therefore the genuinely creative possibility – in the interrelationship of the factors in human selfhood, just as in mathematics, is *there*.

So within the process of our own personhood, just as with the cosmic laws, we have a chance to see the creativity and generosity of God. These are God-created parameters – they are themselves grace and love as well as the means for grace and love and the revelation of grace and love. Of course this is where theologies of personhood, of the nature of the self, diverge radically from theologies of cosmology – because God who is *not* a star, nor a tree nor a poem, *is* a human self, a person, in Christ through the Incarnation.

If Jesus is a self, has personhood as I have tried to describe it, then Jesus has a psychology, a culture, a genetic make-up, gender, a class, a process of becoming – his self too was, to return to Williams's quote, 'a made self', a past acting now. To put it bluntly, the eternal Logos, whose glory we beheld and from whom we have received grace upon grace, was potty-trained – and presumably rather well potty-trained since he did not grow up seeking consolation by conquest, affirming his masculinity over the mother's ownership of his bodily production by despising women, nor having a cringing fear of those in authority. In a sense this may have been one of the things the Lucan narrator was struggling to express in the Annunciation story – Mary's informed consent is necessary because of the social activity that self-becoming necessarily is. The dogma of May's immaculate conception, at least as it is commonly understood, weakens *this* thrust of the story, though of course being a good story it has complex webs of readings and meanings.

The point about all this, is that this view of personhood – this co-creative, deeply social, integrative view – makes much better sense of the Incarnation than a dualist or essentialist one. Firstly it underlines the generosity of God, who really genuinely strips off 'deity' – outsideness, transcendence, necessity – and enters into chance and contingency and risk. Although I actually love the Christmas hymn which begins 'Behold a great creator makes himself a house of clay', I know that in truth it expresses a dangerous heresy. There is *no* still place in the middle of the human being, where the God bit can lurk untouched and uncontaminated.

Such a view of the human person also helps us to understand what is meant by 'incorporation in Christ'. In his becoming a human being Jesus and the rest of us are necessarily incorporated into each other through all the mechanisms I have suggested, and doubtless some others.

Once again, God is not diminished, and indeed cannot be diminished, by an honest investigation into his work as creator. I take this really as axiomatic, but it still seems to need repeating. Actually our real fear is not, and historically never was, that God will be diminished, but that our self-esteem will. Whenever anyone tells you that God is 'endangered' or put at risk by something they are always really talking about their own power-base. A God so frail that she has to be protected from the thoughts that minds created by her come up with is not worth the bother, and I think we all know that. These concepts of personhood may be wrong or right, but either way they will not damage God.

What they may endanger is our arrogant belief in our proper place in the cosmic order. When it comes to personhood, to concepts of the self, to what it means to be a human being, we are all guilty. *Homo sapiens* has spent an inordinate amount of intellectual energy trying to answer the question 'What makes me (and if absolutely necessary, my fellow human beings) special?' Tools were favoured until it turned out that chimpanzees used them; so was speech, and then dolphins posed some delicate questions. And so it goes on. Many of the opponents of artificial intelligence, of the idea that computers might be able not merely to reason as we do but to have consciousness as we do, seem to be motivated by this desire to keep *something* (sensitivity here) as unique to human beings.

Of course it may be that there is something unique about us and that consciousness is what it is; but we won't find this out – if it matters anyway – by holding on to it as a necessity, rather than looking at it with open-hearted delight. If it transpires that human beings are clever enough to create other beings (mechanical, electronic or whatever) that can think and feel and communicate as well as we already can, that says a great deal about our intelligence. Anything that reflects well on our intelligence says some exceptionally interesting things about a creator God clever enough to create that level of intelligence *and* generous enough to give to her creation the extraordinary power and imagination that she herself already has.

As I will elaborate in the next chapter, I think that the creation story which is recorded in Genesis, and the ways we like to think about our origins which grow out of that myth, is particularly nourishing for art and for other creative endeavours. However before I massage my own ego, and I hope yours, by delighting in our creative imaginations, it is important to stress that however good it may be for art, the myth has been demonstrably, singularly bad for *people* (which may well be why so many artists are conspicuously dislikeable and immoral human beings). This creation story makes human beings both special and powerful – made in God's image, having creative power over nature and so on; in addition, unlike pandas and chickens, we are going to get this pure nugget of 'spirituality', this 'soul' which is as eternal as God and is the Real Me, tucked into our hearts or stomachs or brains or wherever it is kept.

It is a naïve idea but I suggest the real answer, in the light of the knowledge we have before us from the created order, to the question 'What makes human beings special'? may very well be 'Nothing, and so what?' We exist by grace and for delight, while we become what we will be. So, it is true that during this century we have learned, or we ought to have learned, that we are not who we thought we were. We are very special but we are not special in the ways that we might choose. This ought not to upset us too much really since narcissism, as we all know, is the way to get drowned.

In the face of these sorts of revelations it has become an intellectual commonplace in some circles, notably but not exclusively theological ones, to announce that our primary feeling or experience as twentieth-century human selves is of 'loss and mourning'. We have had to face a whole lot of uncomfortable facts. There is literally no place on which we can stand outside time and matter and observe the show. It is impossible to argue logically how a transcendent God can go on Being in a cosmos that is so profoundly contingent and yet without boundaries or limits. There is no plausible way that we can think of ourselves as necessary, transcendent, immutable, eternal nuggets of personality, wrapped up in some temporal, non-essential, decay-oriented stuff called flesh. Taken all together these facts can be summed up in the most unpalatable fact of all: God is dead. Or at the very least so contingent as not to be worth bothering about. We are left alone like children screaming unanswered through the night.

Now frankly I can only say that is *not* my experience, *not* what I feel. Having begun with a critique of pure experience it is distinctly dodgy to return to it as a test of the validity of my theology – as Engels made clear, you do not have to *feel* alienation in order to be alienated. Indeed the not-feeling of alienation, of loss and mourning, may be the actual and serious consequence of a very profound alienation. This mechanism of denial is one we are all acquainted with, particularly in relation to death, where people who cannot accept their bereavement and mourn their loss are actually in the most serious emotional predicament. Likewise as a feminist I am aware how much many women do not feel or do deny their very proper anger. So I am constantly struggling to submit my failure to feel much 'loss and mourning' for an older, superficially safer world-view to a rigorous analysis, both theological and psychological. At the same time I have to inspect my profound sense of joy, liberation and hope with a caustic eye. Even having done all that I remain a bit dubious about the need for grief in the face of what we have learned. So, analytically, let me try to ask what it is we are supposed to be mourning; what it is we are supposed to have lost by being forced, kicking and complaining, into a twentieth-century world-view.

We have lost an infantile sense of passivity; we have lost the splendid conviction that the whole universe is a cot in which we are tucked safely and rocked tenderly. While we may scream with hunger and cold it doesn't really matter because the Good Mummy 'out there' (whom for complex reasons of our own we will insist on calling 'the God Daddy') is really looking after us. She has an excellent, indeed perfect, baby manual – and her 'schedule' of meals, playtimes and disciplines will in the long run be good for us.

We have lost both Platonic and Cartesian dualisms – which have allowed us, directly and indirectly, to mess up the planet perhaps terminally and exploit almost everyone on it who does not happen to be white, middle-class and male, or at least good at acting as though they were.

We have lost the romantic and arrogant notion of ourselves as solitary travellers in an alien land, the Great White Hunter, the Nimrod of the cosmos, who eventually, hung with trophies, will go *home* to heaven and patronize the angels. We have lost hero status – the product of bourgeois individualism – which made us feel powerful and made us feel lonely.

We have lost a mechanical saviour doll, who craftily pretended to be just like us while in fact keeping a tight grip on the few privileges of God-ness, of divinity, that we had not already managed to claim for ourselves. He was sent down from heaven by his father to act out the rôle of the suffering servant and make us all feel very guilty. Those of us who felt guilty enough would then be rescued by this *deus ex machina* intervention; be relieved of our troublesome flesh, and allowed to escape from a world whose beauties were but a snare and a delusion. As well as being rather tasteless this was also quite unnecessary, since God was all-powerful and could have redeemed us even more cheaply if he had wanted to.

Of course these are losses – but they hardly seem to call for mourning. Of course this is much easier for a woman to say than a man, because we got to enjoy fewer of the benefits than men did. However even those who did quite well out of the previous arrangement seem to have little to regret, especially in the light of what we have gained on the deal, and at virtually no cost to ourselves.

Firstly, we gain solidarity, incorporation, *love*. We need never be lonely again. We are not only 'bound round in earth's diurnal course with rocks and stones and trees', we are also bound to each other. In reality we are indeed committed to the 'creating of each other's humanity'. We step effortlessly, if we can dare to give up our 'splendid isolation', into the world-view of the Magnificat – where our own vindication necessarily becomes the vindication of all those in need of vindication (the oppressed) and vice versa. I do not stand alone, ever or anywhere.

Secondly, we gain adolescence at least and the hope of adulthood. In the hands of our redeeming saviour God we are of course all children – dependent on grace, on love, on mercy. At the same time, however, within the complexity and generosity of our God, we are also in the hands of *this* creator; and so we are responsible adults too, co-creators, colleagues, friends. Out of this tension is born the pure excitement of adolescence, which is indeed 'very heaven'. I was speaking the other day to a friend of mine who is a schoolteacher and he

was lamenting the conflict between the primary school concept of 'child-centred education' that is experimental, ex-
ploratory, experiential education, and the demands of the
secondary curriculum. He felt that the so-called necessary ex-
amination system meant, in effect, that between the ages of
eleven and twenty all the students' experiments were bogus.
They had to learn only to come up with the 'right' answers,
rather than the true results of their experiments. It made me
think of our new understanding of randomness and co-responsibility. Our creator God has cancelled the exams; our
experiments are for real.

Thirdly, we have gained a possibility of a new and better
expression of the mystery of the Incarnation. Our not-alone-
ness takes on a new dimension: our incorporation – by the
actual nature of what it is to *be* a person – becomes total. God is
committed to the project.

Fourthly, we have restored to us the resurrection of the
body, which, if you can bring yourself to like bodies as much
as God clearly does, is nothing but good news. If there is no
way of being a self, if there is no personhood without material reality (i.e. a body)—with all the elements and parameters
and constructions I have suggested and more—then there is
no resurrection without the body, because there is nothing to
resurrect. The resurrection of the body, as Paul makes clear,
is the ground of our hope and love and joy. It is also a radical demand; or as liberation theologian José Miranda puts it:

> The negation of the resurrection of the dead is an
> ideology of the *status quo*. It is the silencing of the sense
> of justice that history objectively stirs up. It is to kill the
> nerve of the real hope of changing the world. The
> authentically dialectic Marxist and the Christian who
> remains faithful to the Bible are the last who will be able
> to renounce the resurrection of the dead.[14]

The Christian tradition has always known and taught this: that the resurrection is of the body or not at all. The apostolic generation laboured to express it – not just in the peculiar detailing of Thomas probing about in Jesus' wounds, and the repeated insistence that their resurrected Lord *ate* with them, and the reiteration of the empty tomb; but throughout the gospel narratives taken as a whole. In the story of the raising of Lazarus Jesus says to Martha 'Do you believe in the resurrection of the dead?' and she replies 'I believe they will rise at the last day'. 'No', he says, 'I am the resurrection and the life; can you believe this?' and she makes what – under the circumstances – appears to be a very peculiar reply. She says 'I believe you are the Christ; *the one who is come into the world*'. The resurrection, for her, has shifted from a jam-tomorrow spiritual tea party to a present, daily personal relationship, an engagement with the world, with the flesh, with the body. Lazarus stank; his body was real and beloved. Resurrection did not mean for him or for Martha something spiritual, it meant resurrection of the body.[15]

The iconography of the tradition is explicit and sounder than the dubious individualist 'scientisms' of liberal modernism: the resurrected, ascended, glorified Christ, carries, reveals, proclaims always the history-inflicted physical wounds of the passion. He has branded us on the palms of his hands.[16]

We have, I maintain, lost nothing worth mourning in embracing this century's intellectual explorations into the nature of self, of personhood. We have gained a God who is not only cleverer and more subtle than we thought, but also more generous. We can also, if we want to, regain the God of the Old Testament prophets, the powerful and passionate creator God of the pre-Enlightenment. Finally, we have gained for ourselves solidarity, liberation, responsibility and the sure and certain hope of the resurrection.

Notes

1. See Roger Penrose, *The Emperor's New Mind* (Oxford University Press, 1989).

2. Paul Davies and John Gribben, *The Matter Myth* (Viking, 1991), p. 303.

3. Elaine Morgan, *The Descent of Woman* (Constable, 1978).

4. Alla Bozarth-Campbell, *Womanpriest* (Beacon, 1978), p. 41.

5. Athanasian Creed, Book of Common Prayer translation.

6. Anyone not acquainted with this line of argument can pursue it in the writings of, for instance, Rosemary Ruether.

7. Angela West, 'A faith for feminists' in *Walking on the Water*, ed. Jo Garcia and Sara Maitland (Virago, 1984). This article is key to my thinking on this subject, and I believe seminal to socialist feminist theology.

8. Rowan Williams, *Resurrection* (Darton, Longman & Todd, 1982), p. 39.

9. W. B. Yeats, 'Among School Children', stanza 8 in *Michael Robartes and The Dancer* (1921).

10. Peter Middleton, *The Inward Gaze* (Routledge and Kegan Paul, 1993), p. 153.

11. Some palaeontologists recently have not been happy with the timescale: given the age of the planet, there have not been enough generations of many life forms to explain the wide diversity. To speed up the process various ecological crises have been posited. However these theories do not dispute the basic Darwinian claim: the genetic code carried in the DNA mutates randomly, or in response to random biochemical processes like radiation.

12. In other contexts of course it matters very much; which is the whole thrust of all the different feminisms that are expressed in contemporary society.

13. This of course is why the language of parenthood is important in correctly formulating the Trinity. Fatherhood, like the more obvious prototype of motherhood, does not exist without the child. This is how the Son can be co-eternal with the Father: 'there was not when he was not.' There *cannot* be a Father until there is a child.

14. José P. Miranda, *Marx and the Bible: A Critique of the Philosophy of Oppression* (SCM, 1977), p. 146.

15. John 11.1–45.

16. Isaiah 49.16.

3 *Artful theology*

When I originally gave the lectures on which this book is based, I placed this chapter on 'culture' – or ideology, or art – before the one on personhood. It seemed important to stress how profoundly I believe that personhood is created, is constructed within culture; that in a real sense representation, and especially language, precedes personhood; or, more properly, that there is a real chicken-and-egg situation at work. Popular works on evolution tend to simplify this too much. Somehow you have a sense that there was Mrs Naked Ape:[1] feeling too warm in her fur coat, she looks in her evolutionary catalogue and sends off for a nice smooth skin. Later, fed up with the kids fighting all day long, and no longer having nit-picking and fur-grooming as a way of communicating affection and care, she decides that she needs a new means of communication and sends in an order for the language package – which arrives, pre-programmed for regional difference. Of course we know it is not like that, but still we act and talk as though 'human nature' – the self – was a discrete, pre-ordained entity to which ever more sophisticated updatings were added. Whereas, as I have argued, the self is always in the process of construction both within the human lifespan and over the evolutionary aeons; 'the self', to repeat Rowan Williams's beautiful phrase, 'is – one might say – what the past is doing now'.[2] The self is constructed within culture, within ideology, and has no separate ontological reality.

However I have decided to reverse the order, not because I think that the former scheme was wrong but because I have identified a different pattern of thought which makes the first two and the last two chapters 'go together'. In the previous two chapters I have tried to look at what we might learn of God by looking at the state-of-the-art descriptions of what God has revealed in the created order. Now I want to move on and look at what we might learn of God by looking at the creatures' acts of creation – what is it to be a creator? A shift in thinking as it were, from noun to verb.

To be a person is to be a creator. We are all creative, whether we choose to be or not. We all create, by which I mean we all work on the material available and so produce something new; we do it constantly and inevitably. The daily act of eating, digesting and defecating is, as Freud was at pains to point out, a creative act. To make a sentence by combining the words in our vocabulary, in accordance with our understanding of the rules of grammar (rules which Noam Chomsky has suggested are innate), is a creative act. Far from being an amazing mystery, and a complicated and glorious vocation, it is difficult to imagine a human being so malfunctioning that they do not perform a creative act in the course of any given day. This may be one of the ultimate ways in which we are indeed made in the image of God – given the close connection between the word 'image' and the word 'imagination'.

It is because of this conviction that creativity is a natural part of what it is to be a person that I want to look now at the particular acts of creativity which we have culturally chosen to call art. In the last chapter I argued that we *become* persons through our creative acts. I also believe we co-create the material circumstances of our collective future lives by living out the past in the present. This means that it is worth looking theologically at the most self-conscious of our creative efforts, in the hope of understanding more about how our God *is*. We are like God in this, because God lets us be.

What I want to address is the rôle of art seen theologically. I am going to argue that a vibrant and serious attention to the creative arts, and a profound respect for their makers, is a hallmark of a healthy Church – crucial and profoundly theological – because we create in this particular and conscious way only in the light of the creative power of our God.

To do this in a fully incarnational way I ought to be offering you not a theoretical diatribe, but a work of art. I could, for example, simply refuse to engage with any of the genre demands of the theological book and present you with pictures that I think are meaningful – like the picture essay in Berger's *Ways of Seeing*. If the norms of publishing were not so narrow I could have packaged between these pages a CD of music or, better still, a videotape of a performance art group – ideally including jugglers and tightrope walkers: two acts which seem to me to express the psychological stunts of the contemporary Christian lay woman with singular grace. Or, in my case particularly, I could tell you a story or poem. I did in fact try this approach once, with Sue Dowell and Linda Hurcombe. We gave a so-called lecture at the Westminster Centre entitled 'Towards a feminist theology – an experiment' which consisted entirely of readings, songs and slides – highly rehearsed and *performed*. We thought it was fun, but I have to say our audience ratings were poor: people felt baffled and cheated, and I do, if reluctantly, know why. We had called it an experiment to cover ourselves, and as an experiment it was something of a failure.

However apart from this negative response there are other reasons why I am not adopting this approach. One is simple – I have not yet written the fiction that says what I want it to say in this context: it is much harder to write that sort of fiction than it is to write 'proper' theology. This is partly because of my own inadequacies and partly because our society requires consummation from its art. The demands of the genres, the weight of the forms, all push one towards clear resolution. 'Did she go all the way?'

Theologically, however, this consummation is impossible. The infinite is necessarily without closure, resolution or ending. Roland Barthes in his *The Pleasure of the Text*[3] urges us towards the *jouissance* (rather unsatisfactorily translated as 'bliss') of the unresolved text, the ending which opens up rather than closes down. Such texts are painfully hard to write, despite the fact that what we believe about God as the absolute infinite, the uncircumscribed, ought to help us develop open-ended, blissful texts. These are obviously the texts that the great mystics are trying to give us when they write, however clumsily, of reaching the enormous space in which the words fail. Hypostatic union, the feeling of being one with God and therefore in a place/time larger than any words, that is precisely the unconsummated open ending that Barthes is trying to describe.

All this may just be a fancy way of saying that I don't know the answers to the questions I am raising here. It may be that there aren't any.

There is one more quick point I would like to make, a language point. It is difficult to find a satisfactory word to describe what should correctly be called the 'worker in cultural production'. I find that term prissy and unwieldy, as well as not very elegant, not very artistic. However the word 'artist' has become so loaded with both dismissive and, still worse, elitist and culturally exclusive meanings that it is unusable. I am therefore going to use the word 'poet' in place of both the more correct and the more usual words. This is not an accidental choice. The word poet derives from the Greek *poiēts*, which originally simply meant 'maker'. While I use it in this expanded sense it is worth remembering that I am in fact a writer and may well be biased towards that particular linguistic expression of our creativity, as opposed to other forms.

Earlier in this book, when speaking of the cosmological creativity of God, I described God as working more like an artist than like a mechanic (or clock-maker). Once, when I used this image somewhere else, I was asked if this analogy did not in some way deal with the problem of evil: if God is a good artist then she would have to put in 'baddies' as well as 'goodies', shade as well as light, to make a good plot, a good work of art.

Actually my own experience is the reverse of this. It seems to me the more we know of the power and authority and goodness and creativity and artistry of our God, the more pressing, painful and mysterious the problem of evil, of pain and suffering, becomes. Even a little while ago I could not understand, could not begin to enter into, Augustine's huge grief that led him to the highly pessimistic articulation of Original Sin. Now, more and more, I feel I know what he means when his exasperation with Pelagianism explodes into 'Your whole heresy stumbles on the death of a single infant'. Nonetheless the whole question of evil, and whether seeing God as an artist gets around the problem, is very interesting. Or rather it produces all sorts of interesting questions, of which I will raise just two:

(1) Are we humans part of the work of art or the audience, the consumers of it? From inside the work of art I'm not sure that there are goodies and baddies, light and shade in that sense; there are only good ideas or bad ideas. In *Twelfth Night* for example (which I pick because it is a comedy – which is what I believe God is working on, rather than a tragedy – and it's also my favourite Shakespeare play) Malvolio, as a *character*, to the audience, is clearly a 'baddie'; but from the inside of the play, if the play is taken as a whole, he is not a baddie, he is a brilliant idea. He is brilliantly created and is therefore not a bad person but a good thing. I have argued in the two

previous chapters that I do not think it is possible for us to be the audience. We are inside the art work and cannot use its internal structures as the original questioner would like to.

(2)   Is God actually working on a psychological plot, i.e. a modern drama or novel? Both these forms do indeed require heroes and villains. However most art forms, taking a long historical view, do not require goodies and baddies in quite this way. Perhaps God's whole project is a lyrical poem, or a painting, or more like a piece of music. In good musical composition there is tension, and variation and movement, but there is no 'plot' as we would normally understand it; there is no causal, psychological imperative and therefore there is no need for goodies or baddies.

I do think these sorts of questions are worth pursuing, but I suspect strongly that what pursuing them would prove in the end is that we speak of God only in the language of analogy, of metaphor, and that if we press *any* naming of God too far we end up in a whole lot of trouble. Comparing God to an artist is getting it the wrong way round; just as comparing Jesus to a sacrificial lamb, or the Church to a family, or God to a father, is getting it the wrong way round. The right way round is to reverse the process – a lamb may be compared to Jesus; the family may be modelled on the Church; biological fathers ought to behave more like God behaves. We should extend ourselves, from the place where we find ourselves, towards the unlimited God, not reduce that God to the level of our experience. So while I don't think in the end 'poet' completely explains what I believe God is up to, so to speak, I think it might be useful to see the poet as participating in some aspect of God. The language of analogy is a limited language. It happens that, except in the Incarnation of Christ, it is the only language that we have to speak about the unnameable, to speak about God. We must use it or remain silent, but we must use it with caution. David Jones points out the nature of the problem in a sentence so poignant that I use it despite the language:

> Man as a moral being hungers and thirsts after justice, and man as artist hungers and thirsts after form, and although these are ultimately one, because of the truth of that best of all sayings, 'the Beauty of God is the cause of being of all that is' nevertheless for us they are not one, not yet, not by any means.[4]

Nonetheless, hedged around by these doubts and warnings, it is still worth trying to proceed. Apart from anything else there is currently something of a crisis in the whole arena of cultural production. Although it is highly unlikely, to put it in the most optimistic terms possible, that the cultural pundits, or the poetic practitioners of the late twentieth century are going to turn to Christian theology for help, it is still important to see if that theology has anything to say – and if not, why not.

Grand Narrative, we are told, is dead. As far as I can discover the term 'Grand Narrative' was invented simply in order to report its demise. A Grand Narrative is a story, or *the* story, which is of universal relevance: that is a transcendent narrative. Grand Narrative, the theory runs, is now impossible. We are not supposed to be able to tell such stories anymore: everything is relative, so formed by personal experience, coloured to such an extent by cultural imperialism, by gender, race and class, by genre coding and discourse, that the stories collapse under the weight of it all and crawl off into corners to die. All that is left are texts, which may be historical markers, interesting phenomena, but cannot contain and transmit true meanings in the fullest sense. Structuralists take this even further and deny there is any connection at all between the telling and the things told about; between the name and the thing named; between the signifier and the signified: that language has no final meaning. There are nothing but fragments and splinters, there is utterance but no sense, no ultimate connection.

Christianity absolutely denies this. There is, we claim, a universal story. It begins at the beginning (if not before), goes on to the end and then does not stop. There is a Grand Narrative. It is the creative, redemptive and eschatological narrative, centred on the passion, death and resurrection, and developed outwards in all possible directions. It is the workings of God in and with the whole cosmos, and it can be spoken, at least a little, because it has revealed its formal structure in the Word – the creative word and the redemptive word, which (who) is Jesus Christ. If there is any truth whatsoever in our claim, then the idea that God is just a form of artistic expression can and should be reversed: art is just a form of divine expression. The trouble is that too often we trust our own convictions so little that we are actually afraid of art; we prefer abstracted theories to stories, poems and songs because it is easier to fix and control their meaning. We want to fix the narrative and deny the imagination's power. Inevitably we end up with a story littler than it deserves, or littler rather than the God who created it deserves. Very often attempts to enlarge it are not welcomed, but despised; as though adding new stories to our narrative somehow endangered it.

If however we believe our own rhetoric and keep faith with God's Grand Narrative, we can see all art as short stories, contained within the creativity of God; as single poems, single lines or iambs or words of a poem, within a sonnet sequence. Adding to the collection of stories can be nothing other than beneficial, because the activity of creating stories is that of sharing in one of God's activities, literally incarnating an aspect of God, that aspect of the God who is an artist. As an analogy only, I would point to the Bible: if the Bible is seen as Grand Narrative then it contains within it a multiplicity of stories – each book of the Bible is a story, and within that are many more stories – from the complex web of morally repugnant goings-on in Genesis, which somehow surprisingly add up to the account of a magnificent God; right through to the parables of Jesus, each a short story, *not* a theological thesis. Within the overarching narrative of the Bible very complex and peculiar and creative stories can find a shape and meaning which, isolated from the whole narrative, would be either bizarre or disedifying. Within the sweep of the whole narrative, for example, Deborah's glorious song for Jael the Kenite is not *solely* an invitation to radical feminist solutions to 'the man problem'; nor is the story of Daniel a handbook for animal training and jungle survival.

Take for example the story of Abraham, as related in Genesis, chapters 12 to 25. In isolation it is, in the first place, a lousy piece of literature: clumsy, tedious, repetitious and muddled. Incidents clearly garnered from different sources are confused, conflated, reused, but too often not properly integrated. More seriously, since this is supposed to be a story about God's acts for justice, morality and destiny, the material related is full of moral turpitude of such sordid depths that normal concepts of ethics can hardly address it. In particular Father Abraham is, frankly, a real bastard. Among other things he lives off his wife's immoral earnings; he is prepared to bump off his supposedly beloved son in order to please his boss and gain substantial, long-term, material advantages. He is almost certainly insane and demonstrably selfish, autocratic, lecherous, sexist, cowardly, violent and obsessed.

It has to be said that Sarah, our foremother, is not much better. As well as entering with enthusiasm into her husband's schemes for making a quick profit off the Pharaoh by prostituting herself, she also turns Hagar her slave girl out into the desert, with the child she more or less obliged the younger woman to bear, because she is jealous, and because she wants her own son to be his father's sole heir.

This is pretty horrendous stuff, and dressing it up for the

consumption of Sunday school children, and trying to persuade them – and us – that this is in any way an edifying tale
does not make it any better. The point is that this is not the
point. The point is that this is part of an enormous story –
even Genesis, which is only the first of many books in the
Bible, covers an immense amount of ground. This is a small
'human interest' tale within a vast scheme, in which people far
worse than Abraham become necessary to a huge movement,
a Grand Narrative which will take in the whole of history,
indeed the whole of time. We deprive ourselves of a proper
perspective if we try to see Abraham or any of the rest of these
characters as rôle-models. The problem is a problem of scale:
within this Grand Narrative all narratives can be compre-
hended, because it is the ultimate narrative.

Throughout this book I have been trying to find a language
to talk about a Big-Enough God – the God of complexity and
beauty who has so allowed matter to order itself within the
cosmos that (among other things that we do not yet know
about) we may inhabit it with delight, though not always with
safety. This is the activity of God that we have learned to call
the creator; though in this context I want to reiterate my
commitment to the orthodox and traditional view that the
name 'creator' cannot be appropriated to the first person of
the Trinity. In the pursuit of freedom and joy, as well as of
virtue and struggle, we do not want to posit a clock-maker
God, who engineered a deterministic universe, wound it up
and is sitting around observing it slowly running down. We do
not want a creator who, when she noticed the whole thing was
creaking a bit, sent in the Logos, craftily disguised as Jesus of
Nazareth, like an electrician come in to do the annual service.

The outpouring of creation, of the creativity of God, is
continuous; is a continual act, just as redemption is a continual
act and sanctification is a continual act. Indeed they are parts
of the same act; and it is a powerful act, full of power and
glory. Our every breath, like the birth of every star, reverber-

ates to the drumbeat of that power, whether we choose to acknowledge it or not. This is a fact that we often like to forget. We also, of course, like to forget that continuous acts are not without decisive moments: the creation of space/time/matter *ex nihilo* was a decisive moment, just as the Incarnation was a decisive moment.

I also want to claim that this creation is a generous act. The God who acts so, does it with such selflessness that the whole created order is given the power of being instrumental in its own continuing creation – this is called, when we apply it to ourselves, free will. The element of randomness, of chance *and of choice* is inextricably built in. There is of course no obvious logical or moral necessity to interpret it all in this way. In the course of a TV debate about the existence of God, in which I was involved last year, the eminent Oxford physical chemist Dr Peter Atkins argued that God could not exist because if he – Atkins's pronoun, not mine – did, he would be an intolerably lazy God, given how much he left to chance or to mechanistic causality. Apart from the rather curious reasoning which allows someone to argue the non-existence of anything because it has psychological habits that one personally does not quite approve of, it does seem reasonable to argue that God is idle rather than generous. However, if one has been around anyone engaged in a conscious act of creating – of bringing into being that which was not there before – then one knows that it is not a task that can be undertaken with anything other than enormous effort. A lazy God would never have started.

Incidentally, it is important to recognize how much of our own social and moral ethos we bring to supposedly disinterested studies of who or how God is. There is an Inuit tribe who posit a totally incompetent God: not mean or malevolent, but bungling. This God is sound asleep most of the time, and the crucial function of religious ritual is to keep things that way. The priestly task is to sing soothing lullabies, and to urge people not to fight with each other. The noise of disputation and disagreement will wake the God who will, being kindly and well-meaning, want to sort everything out, and chaos will follow. This is one of the few primal myths that lays total responsibility on its adherents: no *deus ex machina* escapes for them. Simone Weil, on the other hand, came to believe that God created by withdrawing, by contracting, by absence. Only in the self-chosen diminishment of her enormous God could there be space for not-God, that is for matter, for time and for space. Creation was precisely where God was absent and did not work.

What Professor Atkins would make of either of these images is hard to guess. It is clear that his idea of God is deeply formed by European Protestantism and its work ethic, to the point that he cannot, in this context, imagine that generosity, love of freedom, desire for collegiality, maternal solicitude or indeed anything other than old-fashioned sloth would cause a loving deity to invite creation to participate in its own making. No wonder he would rather be an atheist than a believer in such a mean, bone-idle deity.

Yet to me the generosity seems on the principle of Occam's razor to be the most straightforward way of describing what I experience. It is a deep level of giving. Within the Roman Catholic Church recently there has been some debate as to whether or not the title 'co-redemptrix' – she who participates in the acts of redemption – can or should be given to Mary. The delicacy of giving Mary such a title is obvious: if the redemptive work is not unique to Jesus, there is a danger of falling into Pelagianism – the 'pull yourself up by your own bootstraps' heresy that so infuriated Augustine. We are saved not by our own good works, but by faith in God's generosity alone. There is also the opposite danger: that we so elevate Mary that we lose all sight of the real and material humanity of Jesus. I have argued elsewhere that if our Marian theology is correctly founded in the slogan 'what we believe of Mary we hope of ourselves', then co-redemptrix, in the light of how and what it is to be persons, is a proper and appropriate title. I am becoming convinced, arguing along the same lines, that 'co-creatrix' is also appropriate: that in our choices and acts we do in fact create the circumstances of our existence and that God consents (if 'consents' is not too passive a word), God *actively* consents to that creative action on the part of the whole cosmos and in particular ways – the ways we have to worry about – on the part of humanity. In Mary we are given an example of how that participation can be perfectly and fruitfully lived out.

Oddly enough the Roman Catholic Church has always recognized this in relation to creative actions of *the Church* – 'whosoever's sins you remit, they are remitted and who-soever's sins you retain they are retained'. God agrees to act along with the Church's collective decision on these matters. Given the extraordinary authority conveyed in this belief it is perhaps sensible of the Church not to confer it too clearly on individual acts. Nonetheless the scientific data that are being discovered in both the hard and the soft sciences do strongly suggest that God's self-giving goes far beyond what the Church has recognized to date. All matter participates in its own becoming. Genuinely new things are thereby brought into being. In the last chapter I spoke briefly about the psychological necessity of Mary's consent driving the narra-tive of the Annunciation in the gospel story. Yes the story has, as I suggested, more general meaning also. The Annunciation story is a poem *par excellence*: 2,000 years have not drained it of interpretive patterning – in pictures, in narratives, in music, in liturgy and prayer, in shadows and frames of other far-distant narratives, the story sustains itself and all its retellings until we almost forget just how good a job the Lucan writer actually has done. We forget to be grateful for his supreme artistry – for it is only a little story and all the theologizing is done elsewhere. Yet that *story*, whose journalistic accuracy is totally irrelevant to its precise truth, has radically affected the movements of history and the formation of personality – for bad as well as good, I might add – for two millennia.[5]

We are called to be co-creators. We live, as I hope I have demonstrated, in the sort of cosmos that encourages the idea of risk and co-creation and freedom. Because we as human beings are blessed with consciousness, our participation in this creativity is necessarily self-conscious: one of the forms it takes is called art. The production of art is quite simply a particular participation in the divine; it is a specific and vital form of theology – defined simply as the capacity to tell stories about the divine, and of course the capacity to hear them – and as Christians we fail to value it at our peril.

Now inasmuch as I see myself primarily as a poet rather than a theologian any thoughts that I have on theology are bound to be, at best, ambivalent, and I think it fair – mainly to myself – to say why. The struggle between the priests and the poets, the theologians and the makers, is very ancient. Plato's philosophic banning of the lying poets from his utopian Republic is only one instance of a long profound psychic struggle.

At the beginning of our known history things were not so. Anthropologists and prehistorians do seem to be in general agreement that the origin of representation was deeply religious in its impulse. The Neolithic communities who painted the walls of their caves with images of the hunt did not do so because of a primitive *Homes and Gardens* impulse to 'redecorate this spring with trend-setting wildlife wallpaper'. They did so because, unlike contemporary structuralists, they believed absolutely that there was a connection between the signifier and the signified, between the image of the hunt and the hunting itself. This connection is now usually called 'magic' but it is a religious, a spiritual impulse. Most of the genres and forms that we have now secularized began in this way: dance and music and painting, almost certainly. Those crafts that may have their roots in practical necessity – such as pottery – were soon co-opted to ritual use. It is, not surprisingly, hard, if not now impossible, to be certain exactly what the purpose of many archaeologically discovered artefacts was. Are the endless little clay 'goddesses' that emerge from the depths of the earth in the eastern Mediterranean really totem images of The Goddess as feminist historians proclaim? Are they fertility fetishes, or even contraceptive icons? But that they had ritual and magical, that is religious, intent is commonly agreed.

For most of recorded history however, and in particular within so-called developed societies, there has been a conflict between religion and cultural production. Most often the clerics have wished to suppress the creativity of the poets: a necessary way perhaps of keeping control not just of the people, but of the gods as well.

This is not a simple matter, and should not be simplified. The ideas that have led people at different times and in different contexts to declare anything sacred, or taboo, or both at once are complex. Making images or representations of these holy things has been, and should be, regarded as risky, and shrouded in mystery, which makes it even harder to understand.

Partly such acts of dedication must have originated in a sort of arrogance: a demonstration to the forces of nature that we puny little primates have power over them; can give them to God, which means we own them in the first place.

Making something sacred, untouchable, unreproducible, is also an act of love, the desire that every lover has to give something to the beloved – something of value. God, the ultimate beloved, has given so much, has given with such profligate abandon, such manic generosity, has given us everything from my fingernail parings to the huge dying red stars out there in space. God's giving is wildly beyond self-interest: it might just possibly be in God's interest that we survive, or even that we are redeemed, but God's giving is excessive – we do not need half God's gifts in order to survive. We do not *need* cauliflowers for example, those entirely superfluous acts of intricacy and creative imagination; we do not *need* the underside of butterflies' wings, or quite so many visible stars; we do not *need* babies' toes to resemble tiny pink peas in pods. The Church of England's Book of Common Prayer sums this up best: we receive from God, and ought to thank God

> for our creation, preservation and all the blessings of this life; but above all for thine inestimable love, in the redemption of the world by our Lord Jesus Christ, for the means of grace and for the hope of glory.[6]

It is quite a package. The desire to give a little something to God, to mark out a small territory and label it 'God only, no admittance', is entirely natural to loving hearts.

There is also the matter of respect, a very sensible caution. The spell-check programme on my word processor, which I have to say is both pagan and right-wing, does not care for the word 'sacred'. Every time I ran this text through the programme it wanted to change the word 'sacred' to the word 'scared'. I know that feeling, I have it; everyone in the Bible has it—they are always 'sore afraid' when they encounter the sacred: the Ark of the covenant, the burning bush, the angelic messenger, the authentic dream. In many societies the act of making something sacred also simultaneously makes it dangerous—you may not touch it, name it, look at it, represent it. There is a fear, and a respect. The proper word is awe. The sacred is awful: it is full of awe. Since the fear of the Lord is the beginning of wisdom there is nothing much wrong (indeed there is rather a lot right) with this feeling, with reminding ourselves of the grandeur, the otherness of God, along with the tenderness and generosity.

Yet even when all this complexity has been acknowledged, there remains the question of power, of power over other people. The naming, or representing, or imaging God directly is a source of power. It is the nature of power that people desire to have it themselves, and they desire other people not to have it. Power corrupts.

The Hebraic mythological stories about Lilith are interesting here. Lilith was Adam's first wife: the wife God made in Genesis 1, when 'God created man in his own image, male and female created he them'. At this point humans were equal, regardless of gender, and were free, without laws. However Lilith and Adam fell out, and interestingly they fell out about male authority. The oldest versions of the story tell that their argument was about what position to have sex in – Lilith complaining about always using the missionary position and wanting to be on top sometimes, and Adam insisting on male superiority. Lilith finally got fed up: despite the apparently ideal living conditions she decided to leave Eden and Adam's petulant sexism. After she had done so, Adam went to God and asked for a different model, one who would admit to his primacy and be obedient. God, with God's usual generosity and willingness to go along with humanity's attempts at creativity, agreed and made Eve out of Adam's rib, as is reported in the second creation story in Genesis 2. The rest, as they say, is history. What is important about this story here is that when Lilith decided to depart she did so by naming God's ineffable name. This gave her enormous power and thus she was able to fly out of Eden and escape into autonomy. She went off to live on the Red Sea coast and re-enters legend – and even, in a shadowy form, the text of the Hebrew Scriptures[7] – as a malignant force, particularly given to the eating of newborn children.

This story is, at the very least, suggestive. In Hebrew culture, naming God's name is so completely taboo that the name itself has now got lost – no one knows what it is: the writing of it was always done without the vowel markers and now it cannot (not merely may not) be spoken. At the time when this story was being patterned, however, it was the priests who knew the name of God, and that was part of their authority. No one else was to name God or even know God's name. Lilith gained immense power by naming God; and she used it to defy the 'proper authorities' – of course she had to be banished and used as a warning to other would-be rebels. God was not to be named, except by the priests. God was not to be imaged in any other way either – the ban on making 'graven images' is not only written into the Mosaic Law, it was also the first of the Commandments that the community broke. Moses was, to put it mildly, badly miffed about that.[8] It is not coincidental that at much the same time Moses also decided to marry outside the law's boundaries. When Aaron and Miriam tried to complain about it, God struck Miriam with leprosy so acute that she 'shone white with the disease':[9] the laws that Moses imposed did not apply to Moses.

The free naming and imaging of God threatens the structures of power, and must therefore be prevented. It is best prevented by restricting the activities of the poets as rigorously as possible – no one must question that the way in which God is described officially is the *only* way that it is proper to describe God. This has led to a prolonged struggle, between priest and prophet, priest and poet, law and charism.

There have, as a matter of record, been times when the poets are the priests, and there have been cultures – one thinks perhaps of the Celtic Church – where an *entente cordiale* has been established at least for a while, but apart from these occasional truces, we see a conflict that has continued over centuries. A very local modern example of this competitiveness is the theologians' almost bizarre failure to seek the advice and comradeship of the poets in the liturgical revisions which have led to the Alternative Service Book and the New English Bible – both of which are quite peculiarly ugly. The

People's Missal – the popular UK edition of the post-conciliar Roman Catholic Mass – did at least try. Collins, its UK publisher, commissioned a series of wonderful woodcuts, many of them calligraphic, from Meinrad Craighead. They are powerful images and it is not meant as a diminishment of them to wonder if there is any significance in the fact that the artist was at that time a nun in an enclosed order. I find myself cynically unable to believe that the Church's hierarchy (a notably clerical one) would have accepted such potent images from anyone outside their control.

My ambivalence now, in the twentieth-century Christian West, however, is based on the fact that it is undeniable that the priests and theologians have categorically won. The poets have been driven out of the holy places and they have suffered from it: one has only to look at the parlous state of the contemporary English-language novel to see how true this is. The poets would not be normal if we did not resent this, if we did not respond with a certain sort of peevishness. It is important, and not just for the sake of a healthy anti-clericism, that we constantly bear in mind that Jesus is both priest and *prophet*: for prophet read poet always.

It is perhaps worth adding that this ambivalence is underscored by my own feminism. Although I am not very interested in labelling qualities 'feminine' or 'masculine', I still have a sense, that is hard to articulate, that the banishing of the artists and the banishing of the women from the scared centres are related. This gives an additional focus to the Lilith story: Lilith is not just *someone* who used the name of God to mount her protest; Lilith is female, a woman, in protest against Adam, who is male, who represents male power. Having already mentioned the Celtic Church as a form of Christianity in which representations, both verbal and pictorial, were produced so freely and to such beautiful effect, it is worth noticing that the Celtic culture also gave *women* a marked degree of both autonomy and authority. Hilda of

Whitby was not just Abbess of a co-ed religious house.[10] She was a woman of great political authority, despite her defeat over the matter of the date of Easter and other Romanizing doctrines at the Council of Whitby in 663/664. In addition, however, to being a determined educator and administrator she was also a great patroness of the arts: it was in her abbey, for example, that Caedmon wrote his beautiful religious poetry – an early example of Anglo-Saxon vernacular verse. I find it impossible to escape the feeling that there is a link between respect for poets and their productions, and a respect for the religious autonomy of women.

This is not, I think, because the two – being female and being a poet – have anything necessarily in common with each other, but because both – for slightly different reasons – are unsympathetic to the intentions of abstracted and cerebral theology. Perhaps this is best expressed by Angela West. In her introduction to a conference of *feminist* theologians called 'The Artful Theology Conference', which was held in Oxford in 1984, she wrote:

> The sources of Christianity are largely without
> abstractions. We have a collection of stories, sayings,
> parables, letters and poems arising out of living
> experience. By sucking out – abstracting – the content
> Western theologians discard context and form as
> irrelevant and clothe them with the trappings of
> philosophical knowledge. All other forms of Christian
> truth are treated as second class. But the biblical texts
> are artful. The Bible's artfulness is our inspiration.[11]

West, here, forges the link that I experience between myself as Christian writer and myself as Christian female. My sense that I am, even as I write this, doubly defeated is real, and it would not be honest to talk about these things without saying so.

In the light of this I would like to look a little bit more at the relationship between God and the creative arts. As I have been saying, we need to get back in touch with the extraordinary imagination and power of God as creator, but I think we then have to go further. Accepting God's creative activity is only a first stage.

We live, as Christians and also as Westerners, shaped by a primal myth about God's creative activity: our God creates by speaking. We are all socially constructed within this myth. It is a myth that has proved so globally successful in terms of colonization and cultural power that it is difficult to remember how unusual a creation mythology it really is. The Children of the Book (and the name is not incidental)—that is, the heirs of the three of the world religions whose roots lie in the cultural drama of the Middle East—are unique. Alone among tribal mythologies we claim to have a God who brought the world, the cosmos, into being by speaking, by words. 'In the beginning God *said* "Let there be light", and behold there was light.'[12]

The hegemony of this narrative makes it difficult to be clear how extraordinary a belief this is. The world is littered with creation myths – prime movers of diverse kinds create the origin of matter, of the world, by ingesting, by laying, by brooding, by birthing, by defecating, by desiring, by withdrawing, by fighting, by coitus, by self-mutilation, by mistake and by means more bizarre than I can list here and now. But by speaking? By externalizing consciousness in this particularly conscious and intellectual way? This is unique. It is also weird.

It is unique and weird in and of itself, but look what comes next. Our story goes on to try something even bolder, even more extraordinary. It gives humanity that creative capacity which in more standard mythologies is confined to the gods alone: human beings are given their authority over the animals, over the world of nature, by being given the power to *name* them. 'The Lord God formed every beast of the field and every bird of the air, and brought them to the man to see what he would call them; and whatever the man called them, that was their name.'[13]

The idea of gift here is important; this is not a Prometheus story, a Loki story, or even a Babel story.[14] Humanity does not steal this power from God, it comes freely and without cost; it is there before the Fall, a part not of evil but of the initial grand plan. Interestingly while Christianity has littered its libraries with debates about whether there was sex before the Fall, it has never thought to question this far more arrogant belief that the creative capacity of language existed in perfection and in 'obedience'.

It is worth pausing to try and imagine what the snow leopard really thought it wanted to be named. Does the panda feel stupid? Does the gnu look so grumpy because of Adam's gaucherie? We know that woman is none too pleased at the derivative and patronizing name her beloved chose for her: a little more sensitivity in Round One could have saved him eons of bother. Perhaps the hen was furious at the dingy monosyllable selected for her – was Adam getting bored by then, she thought, to show so little imagination? Could he not see in her subtle colouring, her orderly fecundity, her amazing voice, a polysyllabic soul? For her it was too late, there she was with Adam speaking, forever 'hen'. (Perhaps, of course, Adam spoke Hebrew or Aramaic or some other language in which the word 'hen' is as exotic, cadenced and beautiful as words like 'syllabub', 'allegro' and 'influenza'. This merely demonstrates the point that the language is central to the meaning of the story.)

It is also worth noticing that there is an odd lapse of logic in this story: the hen, along with everything else, already had a name. She was invented, created, before Adam. God must have spoken *some word*, some name, according to the mythology itself, in order to bring the poor bird into existence, before submitting her to Adam's whimsy. There is a fascinating humility in both God and hen, who put aside their own relationship in Adam's favour.

The society that generated this creation myth must have had a culture full of self-confidence in both its power and its artistry. The invasive military and cultural success of both Christianity and Islam should not really be surprising. Believing in a God like this makes you like a god, a creator, an owner of everything that you name. You have rights and powers over anything that you can name. By naming it you make it, and what you make is yours; as we are God's. Judaism, although clearly capable of concepts of territorial ownership, is restricted from over-aggressive expansion by its inherent concept of specialness, of being a tribally chosen people. Islam and Christianity have no such restrictions: they can incorporate, colonize any cultures that they meet. This is an enormously strong culture, with its huge capacity for self-identity (only one God, how pusillanimous, compared to their neighbours! but they did not care) and zeal (look at the psalmists and be ashamed at the mingyness of your own God's commitments).

When, in the first wave of Christian missionary expansion, this powerful myth encountered the equally verbal but far more sophisticated society of the classical Mediterranean, something extraordinary happened, was bound to happen. The primitive, violently creative, profoundly material speaker of the original word became joined to the concept of the Ideal, united with the Platonic names that are the reality behind all material phenomena. Ah, then indeed The Word became flesh and dwelt among us, full of grace and truth, and we beheld his glory, the glory as of the only Son from the Father.[15] Wow! So strong, so fundamental to our culture is this complex web of power that all the modernist assaults on that myth use as their principle weapon the word 'logical' – that is having the capacity to control the logos, the word. 'Sciential' – meaning to control knowledge – does not exist and 'sophistical' – to control wisdom – is only used derogatively.

That is one way the artist sees the story, and sees with it an obligation to accept a deep responsibility. The flight from the holiness of art has only been a brief post-Enlightenment twitch; has only been the panicked reaction of a people driven out from their own holy places by a colonizing invader. Beautiful on the mountain remain the feet of those who bring good news, which is only a rather better rendering of a very simple statement than Keats's Grecian urn's more amoral version: 'Beauty is truth, truth beauty; that is all / ye know on earth and all ye need to know.'[16]

Another response to the biblical story that you might get from a poet is slightly different. It is 'Oh, wow'. It is 'What a great *story*'. It would be to turn to the theologians and say 'What, in God's name, do you think you are up to?' This latter response is best expressed by the American philosopher O. K. Bouwsma in his essay in Richard Bell's book. Here he examines the possibility of 'proving' the existence of God and he ends up saying, and I paraphrase:

> Of course you can prove the existence of God; it is quite
> an amusing thing to do any afternoon between lunch
> and mowing the lawn. And at the end of it what sort of
> God have you proved the existence of? The sort of God
> that you *can* prove the existence of. Was it for this that
> Abraham went out from Ur of the Chaldees, a very
> pleasant place to bring up the children?[17]

I shall use my own privilege here and tell you a personal story which makes, I think, exactly the same point from a rather different perspective. I have told this story elsewhere but will risk telling it again because it seems to me such a perfect contemporary parable:

A few years ago, just a day or so after York Minster was

struck by lightning, I was on my way to the local post office near my home, which is in a wretchedly poor part of Hackney, when I met an elderly woman. She was most distressed by this bolt from the heavens, this Act of God as the insurance people call it (which alone gives you pause for thought). She was very upset. Did I think, she asked, that God had done it on purpose, as some of the newspapers were speculating? The post was about to leave and I was in a hurry, but how can anyone resist such a subject? No, I said, I didn't really think so, did she? No, she said, she didn't really think that God was like that. There was a pause and I was poised to escape. Then she added, in what I can only describe as a tone of affectionate criticism, 'But he should have been more careful, he should have *known* there'd be talk'.

I think this is delightfully funny, but it is more than just funny: she is talking about God as the Hebrew Scriptures talk. This is the God of Abraham, the God of the Psalm writers. It is also the God of *A Dream of the Rood*, the young warrior who hastens eagerly to the conflict:

> Then I saw the King of all mankind,
> In a brave mood hasting to mount upon me.
> Refuse I dared not, nor bow, nor break,
> Though I felt the earth's confines shudder in fear;
> All foes I might fell, yet still I stood fast.
> Then the young warrior, God the All-Wielder,
> Put off his raiment, steadfast and strong;
> With Lordly mood, in the sight of many,
> He mounted the Cross to redeem mankind.[18]

This is not a new modern trendy vision of the deity at all. I believe that this is the God who called Lazarus from the grave in the knowledge that indeed he was already stinking.

This is the God of the horsehair worm, and the lightning bolt – not a petty-minded headmistress thinking up intelligence tests and morally improving games for me. We know it isn't like this. Those of us who have had the privilege of loving know that we do not look into the eyes of our beloved, of our children, of our friends and say 'What are you for? To what moral edification or theological revelation can you be put?' We say 'I love you', and if the angels cheer so much the more fun for the angels. Now as it happens if we love we will gain moral edification and theological revelation and the angels will cheer, but I know that sure as hell that is not what loving is for. I do not want a God whose love is less generous than my own pale imitations of it.

God is not careful. Theology is careful, and it ought to be; but God is not careful, is not bound by rules. This double-dealing magic-weaving careless God, this God of strange codes and complex twistings of imagery and power, this God whose sense of humour so often seems to outweigh any sense of ethical propriety, this playful God: this is the God of the artists.

I want to be clear here. I am not contrasting the God of law with the God of chaos – that is a different story altogether, though certainly one worth telling. I am not contrasting the first person of the Trinity, God as creator, with the second person of the Trinity, God as redeemer, because that would be unorthodox and inaccurate. There is after all nothing more incarnational than art: it has no abstract existence whatsoever. There is nothing chaotic about the work of the good poet. If you ask any poet what is their most hated social response to their work, nine out of ten of us will tell you it is the person who says 'I've always felt that I had a great book (or picture, or tune) inside me'. There are no great books inside people: *what it is to be a book is to be outside people*, to be a separate physical entity. Until it is written down by a steady and laboriously con-crete process it does not exist at all. This incidentally is why Dorothy Sayers's heroic attempt in her book *The Mind of the Maker,* to describe the Holy Trinity by analogy to the writer's work, finally fails – even though her 'finally' occurs long after most of us have stopped trying. She needs there to be something she called The Idea of the Book to represent the Father, but I am certain that all art, like the Incarnation itself, does not exist in this way. The message and the messenger are one and the same.

No, this is not about contrasts, but about modes. Here we have an enormous God about whom we can say very little because there is too much to say. It is the job of both the Church and the poet to try to structure that enormity intellectually and emotionally, both to contain and to reveal it. Form it is called, form and structure and genre. I cling to orthodoxy in theology and to form in cultural production. The challenge is to go as near to the edge, as near to the power and the mystery and the danger without collapsing into chaos. Neither the Church nor the poets seem to be working too well at the moment; the people 'drift and die', we are left shepherdless catching at fragments as best we can. Much art seems to be either anarchic or omphalosceptic[19] – most serious novels are about the intellectual agony of writing novels, which is not much use. Much 'church' seems to be simply boring – too many services are about the intellectual agony of how to do services, which is not much use either. The only bits that stick with most people are the hymns, actually, and that should not be surprising – they are made by poets and musicians, not by theologically expert liturgical committees.

I blame the Church. The Church really hates creative imagination, especially if they can't understand it or don't know what it is *for*. (As I have already said, most Christians have an appallingly functionalist view of themselves and all their activities.) When the Church is confronted by some kid who has spent hours of time and labour and energy creating a new thing out of base matter – out of her hair, out of carpet dye and scissors and a razor blade; who has changed boring safety pins into jewels; who has pricked out the equivalent of the Sistine Chapel ceiling indelibly and painfully onto her skin, who has in short acted as God with the only matter that she owns: her own flesh – the Church does not usually welcome her with an 'Oh wow', does not thank her for being in a tiny way 'like God' and praise her as one who reveals potential. When good, nice Christians see the young romantic poets of our generation, people who will literally risk life and limb for the sake of their art, the graffiti artists, we do not usually think 'Well, we have acres of boring old wall, and here is someone with nearly as manic a sense of colour as God showed in the making of the Vermont autumn'.

I am not saying that much punk is not nihilistic and aggressive; I'm not saying that for many graffiti artists the impulse is not to destroy. Indeed, my husband once sat on a bus and listened with some surprise to two thuggish-looking youths complaining about the particularly ugly graffiti which adorned the walls. 'Nobody seems to care', they complained. He was smiling with clerical approval at their civic concern when one of them added 'I mean look at that, it must be a good three weeks since I put it on and no one has even tried to clean it off'.

I am not naïve, and I do not want to romanticize squalor, but I do want to complain about a churchy habit of mind that believes that art is threatening before it even looks at the art.

At a more controlled level you might well think that at the very least (and leaving out, for a moment, all the justice issues and the bias to the oppressed issues) the Church would fall with delight on feminist discourse which has unknotted a nonsense. Feminist creative theology has demonstrated that the expression 'Of course God isn't male or female, of course he is both' is simply rubbish, is non-sense, is a non-sentence. By declaring it a non-sentence, and by establishing there is no sentence that can replace it, feminist theologians have creatively given back to us the simple orthodoxy that 'God is

without qualities' and in addition have exposed the unname-
ableness, the vastness of God, who sustains divine personhood
out beyond the frontiers of our grammatical rules. You would
think that the most conservative, most strictly orthodox
theologians would be over the moon with gratitude at this
useful logical intervention. But are they? Are they hell – to use
a vulgar phrase in a carefully constructed context.

This feminist-inspired business of creating (inventing?
discovering? I am not sure of the vocabulary here) an inclusive
language, a new grammar to speak about God, ought to be
seen as one of the most interesting theological engagements
that is being undertaken at present. Much of this work has
been illuminating, mind-and-heart-expanding.[20] It is not
always successful; but even when it fails it is creative, because
the inadequacy of new articulations renews and revitalizes the
older turns of phrase. For example, many of us feel that the
trinitarian formula 'Father, Son and Holy Spirit' is not totally
satisfactory because it appears to assign gender to God, who is
of course without gender. It can even feel clichéd and lazy.
However the attempts to suggest non-sexist alternatives have
demonstrated just how sophisticated that particular formula
is, and how difficult it is to express differently. For instance,
'Creator, Redeemer and Sanctifier', probably the most popular of the new forms, may not assign gender to God, but it does
allocate functions (jobs no less) to each of the divine persons.
This divides their unity, in a way which the original deftly
avoids. Both the second and third persons are involved in
creating with the first person; the first and third persons are
necessary to our redemption; sanctification is not the sole
prerogative of the third person. Or, as the Athanasian Creed
puts it, it is important that we find ourselves 'neither con-
founding the persons nor dividing the substance'. There has
been little recognition of the benefits of inclusive language,
not merely as consolation for women (not that there should
be anything 'mere' about expressing solidarity with the

oppressed) but for everyone who wants to articulate our faith more clearly.

Instead, most of this work has been met with an extraordinary level of hostility. Indeed it is this aggression which makes me certain that feminist theologians are on to something exciting: no one minded Gerard Manley Hopkins calling Jesus a 'windhover' after all. The trouble with banning books and shouting at women who are struggling to name God is that it makes their task more difficult to do, even while enforcing in them the idea that it is important. It is hard to make something beautiful in the face of this bossy din, this incessant nagging.

In the last chapter I said that I did not know of any Christian feminists who denied the Fatherhood of God – only those who wanted to extend the list of analogies, to work creatively in the space between our personal relationships with God and the tradition that has given us a language through which to meet God. This walking along the very edge of the cliff of the possible is a courageous and creative place to be.

And yet, even to think this way feels risky. Surely we are not meant to believe that *everything* that can ever be said about God has been said, let alone has been said by theologians. I will tell you just a few things about God which no 'real' theologian would ever have dared to tell us; indeed could not have told us—and that is without going to the grand canon of poets who knew they were also theologians, without applying to the late psalmist or Dante or Milton or Manley Hopkins or even Chesterton:

> 'On with it?' He says, and thus
> We squat by the sea
> and play – can it be true –
> a game of poker.
> He calls me.

I win because I hold a royal straight flush.
He wins because He holds five aces.
A wild card has been announced
but I had not heard it
being in such a state of awe
when He took out the cards and dealt.
As He plunks down His five aces
and I sit grinning at my royal flush,
He starts to laugh,
the laughter rolling like a hoop out of His mouth
and into mine,
and such laughter that He doubles right over me
laughing a Rejoice-Chorus at our two triumphs.
Then I laugh, the fishy dock laughs
the sea laughs. The Island laughs.
The Absurd laughs.

Dearest dealer,
I with my royal straight flush
love you so for your wild card,
that untameable, eternal, gut-driven ha-ha
and lucky love.[21]

That is Anne Sexton, who killed herself very soon after she had written it. And here is Michelene Wandor:

Abstract art must truly be divine
for did not the Lord say

'Thou shalt not make unto
thee any graven images or any likeness
of any thing that is in heaven above
or that is in the earth beneath
or that is in the water under the earth'   Exodus 20:4

gold and silver and brass
blue   purple   scarlet   linen
goat's hair
        oil for light   spices for anointing oil
incense   onyx
            emerald   sapphire
diamond   agate   amethyst

blue lace
            bread and lamb

my burnt offerings
my tabernacle, my temple: art

myrrh   cinnamon
olive oil

frankincense
            stone tablets
pillars of cloud and fire

Shining faces
almonds   flowers

Oh God.[22]

Neither of these poets would see themselves as religious. They
would deny it hotly. What religious experience have we been
teaching that denies that any act of creation is other than a
religious act, other than a participation in the divine Grand
Narrative, in the holy acts of God? I had an argument the
other day, with a very nice and I think very clever priest. He is
a form critic. We argued because he would not acknowledge
that imagination had any part to play in biblical interpretation. We didn't get very far. I said I wanted him to do his job

well so that I could do mine better; I wanted him to give me the best text, best contexted, so that I could play with it. He said I was the sort of person who believed in the virginity of Mary on the basis of a mistranslation from the Old Testament prophets: did I imagine, he enquired, perhaps a little sarcastically (we were both getting heated), that St Luke was lurking behind a pillar when the archangel arrived, with a tape recorder in his pocket? I said he was the sort of person who wanted to replace a Luke behind a pillar with a form critic in her bed. He said, not unreasonably, that I was cheating. I said I was being imaginative. He said that imagination only distorted the text. I said that they were imaginative texts to start with, so how could imagination distort them? He said and I said and he said and I said, you know how it goes. In the end he said 'Either we can talk about theology or we can talk about creativity; we can't talk about both together'. I wanted to cry.

What have we done? This rejection is terribly dangerous to the poets. We must understand that. This is more an appeal for readmission to the sacred groves than it is an accusation. It is dangerous in two directions, both of which have theological implications.

In the first place, excluded from the central source of creativity many of the poets have felt forced to set themselves up as 'rival creators', in competition with God, as George Steiner pointed out in his otherwise somewhat tiresome book *Real Presences.*[23] Mary Shelley (notable as one of the very few human beings privileged to have actually created a real myth herself) made us imaginatively aware, even before Hiroshima made us politically aware, of the dangers of rival creators. Art was never meant to be a substitute for religion, only a particular expression of faith and joy. During the crucial cultural debate which arose after the publication of his novel *The Satanic Verses*, Salman Rushdie said something extremely interesting. (It is important to remember how profoundly theological the whole debate around that book was, or would have been if we theological folk had dared to find any language to engage in it.) Rushdie said that he had a 'God-sized hole' in the centre of himself that he had to fill up with literature. If that were not tragedy it would indeed approach blasphemy. Poets do not really want, although rejected and maimed we may think we want, to be rival creators; we really want, and need, to be co-creators.

This is not just a proper humility, it is also necessary to the task. With all due respect to Jung, symbols – recognized patterns of meaning – are not ahistorical, transcendent idealist absolutes. They are socially constructed. But they are not abstracts, purified essences of experience or meaning, they are constructed within contexts, and the contexts are *narratives*, as Russell Hoban so powerfully demonstrated in *Riddley Walker*[24] (one of the most glaring exceptions to my wholesale condemnation of the contemporary novel – it ought to be compulsory reading for all Christian catechists, broadly understood). Christians know this of course – it is one reason, however unconscious, why the eucharistic prayer always contains the narrative, the story, of the Last Supper, even though this has created considerable theological confusion. The fact remains that you can't just wave a chunk of not very convincing looking bread about and expect everyone to 'get it' straight off. The bread and the wine, or the water of baptism, or the cross itself for that matter, have no 'pure' meaning; they are given their meaning by the stories which make them, place them, frame them. Which, not incidentally, is why the theory that signifiers – words – have no connection to the signified – objects – is wrong. However casual or random the association may have been originally, usage, history – that is time in the genuinely creative, poetic (*making*) sense that I explored in the first chapter – has given them meaning, real meaning, by placing them within sentences of meaning, placing these symbols of meaning within narratives which carry that meaning.

If the theologians want to fix, dogmatize, both the narratives and the narratives' meanings there is simply no studio within which the poets can work. They have to go off and construct their own without reference to any more general patterning. This frequently proposed and stupidly glorified task of creating individual, isolated tales from our own 'personal, bodily experience' cannot but leave us with fragmented and personalized complexes of images, rather than shared and collective patterns of meanings. Nor are there any clear indications as to how these complexes might communicate with each other within social structures.

The second danger is the flip side of the arrogance of the first, and may explain why so much contemporary 'Christian' art is so mawkishly sentimental. If poets want to stay within the cultural boundaries of faith, if they know that they need that succour, that nourishment; then they have to pay for it by accepting the often rigorous limitations that the priestly authorities choose to impose upon them. The trouble with such compulsory grovelling is simple: it is nearly impossible for a halfway good poet to make anything decent while lying, while not feeling free to speak the truth. I have to say that I am not at all sure why this is so. It is not self-evident that fiction has to be based on a personal truth. For some reason the effort of going into the metaphorical mine, the place where the treasure of meaning is kept, and hacking out one's own meaningful version is enormous. Even the original creator seems to have found creation tiring work, because on the seventh day God rested. Experience seems to demonstrate that it is impossible to do that exhausting thing while simultaneously censoring oneself. By and large religion has failed to acknowledge this and continues to want to instruct poets as to what truths they will make. Poets who try to work within these boundaries, for whatever reason, fear or obedience or laziness, cannot really produce something new, something real, because the new necessarily lies outside the boundaries which mark the line between what we have already tamed and the wild.[25] *Veritatis Splendor*, the recent papal document on moral theology and its limitations, reflects this rather churchy habit of mind when it says of course theologians should ask questions, but they have to come up with the right answers. This is dubious at best; but it is quite impossible when one is dealing in areas of creativity, where one cannot know in advance exactly what the question *is*, never mind whether there is a right answer.

Yet the dangers of the dismissal of the poets are wider than this. I am not arguing solely for the benefit of poets, but on behalf of all of us. The real danger of not treating the creative imagination with real love is that this involves a rejection of God – or at least of a huge and magnificent dimension of God. Such a rejection seriously impedes the work of religion in the transformation of the world. Any movement for social change requires a revolution of the imagination; and for that, perfect theory is not good enough. There have to be stories told afresh, rhythms created anew, meanings presented to the heart. That is what Jesus' parables are: they aren't just mnemonic aids to good behaviour; they are new stories, which construct truths afresh. As Keats says, 'Axioms of philosophy are not axioms until they are proved upon our pulses'.[26]

All these doubts about and deep fears of the poets help to explain many of the problems that seem to beset us now. Propositional logic allows for only two positions: true or false; and for no internal contradictions: 'If A then not B' is the classic expression of this. However not everything consents to fall under the laws of propositional logic – even, as I showed in Chapter 1, propositional logic refuses to obey its own rules. One of the many things that absolutely refuses to be bound to such limitations is God. The poet's job is to speak the language of unlimitedness, to stand in the place where the rules are different: 'If possibly A, then why not maybe B as well', 'If A and B, then also C' and so forth. Some things can be controlled and should be: for example, it is a good thing to decide on which side of the road people should drive their cars and then do everything you can to make them keep to that side only. Some things cannot be controlled and trying to control them is not only impossible but exhausting: for example, staying awake to control the content of one's dreams would be not merely futile but also damaging. If we could respect the prophets and the poets as we respect the priests we would relieve the tension that exists, for instance, between charismatic and ordained ministry. We could ease the apparent opposition between science and religion; the polarized understanding of gender; and the confusion around how 'political' spirituality can or should be. 'Either/or' say the logical minds, and rightly. 'Both/and' say the poets, 'I don't know, but what if . . . ', and equally rightly.

I seem to be getting a bit functionalist myself here. None of these is what art is *for*; ultimately it is for delight, for joy at the most serious level, it is for love and continuity and solidarity. It is for complexity and mystery. There's a nice story about the desert father who argued that all images for God were only metaphors, that none of them described God at all and many limited her. His inquirer asked him why he went on trying to talk about God and he said 'Why does the bird sing?' As it happens, since the days when he was lurking out in the desert, we have learned that birds sing for some pretty functional reasons: to protect territory, to seduce the opposite sex, to summon their young or their chums, to intimidate their competitors and so on. Yet still the heart leaps up at bird song, still there is a surge of delight, still there is a joy in knowing that even in the forests where there are no ears to hear the birds sing.

I have been reading Richard Niebuhr's *Christ and Culture* recently in an attempt to get some handle on this. His five categories of the possible relationship between Christ and culture are interesting in themselves, and I commend them to your consideration, but what is most interesting in this context is his conviction that none of them is exclusively right; that all have bearing and do not eliminate the others. This is a very rare posture for a theologian to take up. It is absolutely the position taken up by fiction writers.

It is openness that we need, and we can only find it if we develop our faith in the power of our Grand Narrative: if we truly believe that it is a huge strong story, and we will be more than ready to welcome new tellings of it, short stories added on or tucked in within its folds. We can only find that confidence – a word which simply means 'with faith' – through welcoming back the tricky and alarming workers of ambivalence.

We need jugglers and high-wire artistes – sequinned, sparkling and dancing on the void – if theology is to measure up at all to the magnificent God whose gambling habits and sleights of hand boggle our simple minds. We need a deeply imaginative meditation on the narratives and symbols of our past if we hope to co-create a future. We need a powerful vision of the beauty of God and the beauty of her creation; not false prophets who cry peace, peace when there is no peace; but those who will ride the wild storm cloud and hide in the clefts of the rock just to see the hinderparts of God. We won't get any of this until the poets are embraced and allowed, encouraged, loved into running all the risks they want.

At the beginning of this chapter I said that I would not use an artful form to try and explain what I meant by the business of art and the divine, but now, at the end of the chapter, I will tell you a story.

I often dream I am a tightrope walker. I climb the rope ladder slowly, carefully, adjusting to its wrigglings. The wooden slats mutter to me all the way up. The rungs my right foot stands on say 'If you are afraid of falling, you will fall', and the rungs my left foot presses say 'If you believe you cannot fall, you will fall'.

Eventually I arrive on the little platform at the top. I strip off my track suit and am revealed in all my sequinned glory. I look out and down at the upturned eyes, sparkling brighter than my costume. Then the spotlight pins me, and I hear its mocking tones.

It says 'And probably in the end you will fall anyway'.

And in my dream, I always listen politely and know it is true, and then I go out sparkling, flashing and dance on the void. That is the challenge, the moment of hope: to dance as near the edge of destruction as is possible, to be willing to fall and still not fall. And the audience cheer, because it is beautiful and because they know that this time I may indeed fall and because they know that that is precisely why it is beautiful, and I have made it beautiful.

That is a good dream.

I believe we need a more artful theology.

Notes

1. Mrs Naked Ape is not, alas, my own invention, but Elaine Morgan's in *The Descent of Woman* (Constable, 1978).

2. Rowan Williams, *Resurrection* (Darton, Longman & Todd, 1982), p. 39.

3. Roland Barthes, *Le Plaisir du texte* (1975); translated by Robert Miller as *The Pleasure of the Text* (Cape, 1976).

4. David Jones, *Art in Relation to War* (1942), p. 134.

5. It is important not to overlook, for example, feminist difficulties with parts of this narrative. In *Pure Lust* (Beacon, 1986), Mary Daly spells out the elements of spiritual – and actual – rape in this story; pointing out that the Immaculate Conception means only that at the Annunciation Mary has no power to say no, to refuse this impregnation. She has had her free will stripped away; and holding her up as a rôle model for other women actively encourages rape, and the notions of female passivity. This does not seem to me a totally viable reading; nonetheless Daly correctly analyses the way in which Marian doctrine has been used against women. It is important to keep in mind, and I do not want to suggest otherwise, that even great art, divine art, can be used and abused and put to functionalist ends – from exploding the power within the atom over Hiroshima, to the bowdlerizing of children's nursery rhymes. That is power.

6. The General Thanksgiving, Matins, Book of Common Prayer (1662).

7. Whenever you encounter a screech owl in the Bible, it is Lilith lurking disguised.

8. Exodus 32.15–26.

9. Numbers 12.10.

10. It is interesting how often the mixed religious houses, quite common in northern Europe until the Middle Ages, were led by women. Hilda was not exceptional in this. St Walburga, one of Boniface's companions in the conversion of Germany, is another example – preserved in memory because of 'Walpurgisnacht', the German parallel to our Halloween.

11. The Artful Theology Conference, Oxford, 1984. The pamphlet introducing the day, which contains, *inter alia*, this passage, is preserved with other archival material in the CWIRES collection in the theological library of Manchester University.

12. Genesis 1.1–3.

13. Genesis 2.19.

14. Prometheus, in Greek mythology, stole fire from Olympus to give to humanity: it is for this presumption that he is pinned forever to a rock while birds of prey pluck out his bowels. Loki, in Nordic myth, is a strange figure, a god who is both naughty and bad – he constantly stole various treasures, material and spiritual, from other gods and it is his constant mischief that puts the gods, and the virtuous who will fight with them, at real risk of defeat at the final battle of Ragnarok.

15. John 1.14.

16. John Keats, 'Ode on a Grecian Urn', stanza 4 in *Endymion* (1818); W. H. Auden points out in *The Dyer's Hand* (1962) that it is not Keats himself, but the urn. The poet takes a critical stance in relation to this aesthetized morality.

17. O. K. Bouwsma cited in R. Bell and R. E. Hustwit (eds), *Essays on Kierkegaard and Wittgenstein* (College of Wooster, Ohio, 1978); originally in J. L. Craft and R. E. Hustwit (eds), *O. K. Bouwsma: Without Proof or Evidence* (University of Nebraska Press, 1984), 'Zettel 2'.

18. From *A Dream of the Rood*, author unknown, *c.* 750–800. Translated by Charles Kennedy, in *An Anthology of Old English Poetry* (Oxford University Press, 1960), p. 145.

19. This is a real word: it means, as the context suggests, excessively introspective – in origin 'examining/inspecting one's own navel'. I have long thought it a lovely word and I have wanted to have a chance to use it. So despite editorial protests, I am doing so here.

20. The creative works of both Janet Morley and the St Hilda Community will show just how lovely, in the fullest sense of the word, such worship material

can be, and how even the apparently simple task of changing gender creates new and challenging patterns of meaning. At one of the first large services presided over by one of the earliest of the US Episcopal Church's women priests, the processional hymn was 'Come labour on' (a hymn often used for the first Eucharist of a newly ordained priest in the USA). The word 'labour' alone carried a whole new layer of meaning when it was sung in celebration of the ministry of a woman.

21. From Anne Sexton, 'The Rowing Endeth' in *The Awful Rowing Toward God* (Houghton Mifflin/Chatto, & Windus, 1977).

22. Michelene Wandor, 'Lilith in the Morning' in *Gardens of Eden: Poems for Eve and Lilith* (Journeyman/Playbooks, 1984), p. 4.

23. George Steiner, *Real Presences* (Faber and Faber, 1989).

24. Russell Hoban, *Riddley Walker* (Cape, 1980).

25. The expression 'beyond the pale' is useful here. 'The pale' was the fence (as in the modern word 'palings') or boundary between the bit of Ireland that the English Crown had under control, and the wild bit beyond which it did not. Going beyond the pale meant moving into wildness – heavily weighted with ideas of treason and going over to the enemy.

26. Keats, letter to John Hamilton Reynolds (3 May 1818).

4 Angelic woodlice and other delights

Philosophy is odious and obscure,
Both law and physic are for petty wits,
Theology is basest of the three
Unpleasant, harsh, contemptible and vile,
'Tis magic, magic, that hath ravished me.[1]

Recently someone told me a joke which seems relevant to the topic under discussion: What is the difference between 'involvement' and 'commitment'? It's like bacon and eggs: the hen is involved but the pig is committed.

In the preceding chapters I've tried to demonstrate, through an exploration of a variety of contemporary disciplines, my conviction that the best available state-of-the-art data give us a vision of a God who is definitely more pig than hen. He is not *just* – though there should be nothing but awestruck amazement even in that 'just' – at the human historical level, but likewise at the primary, the deepest levels; the level of creation and creativity, the level of how-it-really-is. God is committed, is inextricably bound into contingency, into matter, materiality and chance. I have also suggested that far from this being a recipe for despair – for 'loss and mourning' – it is indeed good news, in fact the Good News, news of liberation and hope, at least for those of us who want to be grown-ups – or, perhaps I should say, for those bits of all of us that want to be grown-ups.

I have tried to share my belief that Christianity, faced by a science it did know how to address, has made a cowardly retreat over the last few centuries into a defensive posture that has abandoned the large-scale and shrunk God down to a well-adjusted super-ego, or to the senior line manager of a business called Established Religion plc (stress on the L for 'limited') whose product can best be summed up as 'morals tinged with emotion'. This retreat has been quite unnecessary, unjustified and unorthodox; and has been the product of both fear and arrogance.

So, as it turns out, we do not have a little tame domestic God, thank God, but we do have a huge, wild, dangerous God – dangerous of course only if we think that God ought to be manageable and safe; a God of almost manic creativity, ingenuity and enthusiasm; a Big-Enough God, who is also a supremely generous and patient God; a God of beauty and chance and solidarity.

Now I want to move on to look at some of the consequences of a belief in such a God, and I do this in the honest belief that there is no other credible God: it is a God as big and unmanageable as this or no God at all – only the whimperings of an individualist liberal humanism, or a brave but harsh stoicism in the face of crude materialism, red in tooth and nail, busy going nowhere. I want to ask myself some 'so what?' questions; to look at some of the demands, if you like, that such a faith might make on us – as people who are *made selves*, who are these kinds of persons, part of *this* cosmos, in *this* particular time and space. If there is any content whatsoever to this idea of matter – and ourselves as part of and within matter as co-creators, makers daily of the 'brand new thing' that we call the present, then ethics are important in a slightly more pressing and demanding way than we have been led to think. How we act and react is, in a true sense, what we make; and if we make it badly, falsely, selfishly, then that is how it will be. We will have to live in, and hand on to the future generations, a bad, false, selfish world – or at least, since we are not the sole creators, a worse, falser, more selfish world than it might otherwise be.

Unfortunately there is a well-explored and still intractable philosophical problem in trying to argue an 'ought' from an 'is'. My argument, that creation is contingent and risky and may well, like Scripture and tradition, be already committed through history and sin, makes the problem worse. I have already warned of the dangers of using the created order in the way that biblical and ecclesial fundamentalists have used Scripture and tradition – a danger into which it seems to me that a good deal of contemporary 'creationist' and 'experiential' theology too lightly tumbles. We have to learn to see the whole of the created order (and of course there is no other order and nothing except God outside that order) more as a living, and therefore growing and changing, organism; more like a 'self' as defined in my second chapter than a static absolute.

However valuable it is, this perception undeniably makes the logical movement or path between the 'is' of the universe and the 'ought' of ethical conduct even more tenuous and tricky than it was when we thought we were working with some tidily ideal forms of the Platonic variety. Our bones may indeed be the dust of the old red stars, in fact they demonstrably *are*, but it is hard to forge an inevitable logical connection between that fact and how, say, I *ought* to vote tomorrow. I repeat, it is notoriously unsafe to try and conclude an absolute 'ought' from a contingent 'is'; to try and read off ethics from physics, or in this case from metaphysics.

In a sense about the only conclusion we can easily draw from most of the material I have been examining is that God is stunningly and impressively clever, and whichever way we wriggle we come back to that cosmic intelligence. If, for instance, it turns out that personhood is entirely built within neutral networks, electronic machinery, then we have a God who can create neural networks so intricate and elegant and competent that we don't believe that that can be enough. We feel that there ought to be something more; we cannot really accept *that* story as adequate, as good enough. This is a brainy, a brilliant God, but this fact hardly leads to very obvious ethical directives, except of the most banal kind.

Of course this need not mean that we cannot draw any moral conclusions, ethical imperatives, at all; it means only that this contemplation of God as creator may not prove the place whence to draw them. I began this book with the absolute proviso that I believed in, that I took my stand, not on logical necessity but on revelation: that we know nothing of God except what God chooses to give us. There are a variety of types and forms of revelation. There are all sorts of places whence we can draw ethical concepts and against which we can test such concepts and rulings. All I am trying to say is that we may not bully the data.

It is vital to remember that *it* – that is, everything which is, including of course ourselves and our experience – is not necessarily here just to instruct us and inform our moral sensibilities. We must be very careful not to treat God's (or our own) creativity in a purely functionalist way: it quite possibly is not like that, is not for that. It seems to me, at the very least, that whatever God's motives for making matter, and becoming committed to this whole enormous process, it cannot have been simply and solely to enable a few human beings to work out whether or not it is morally desirable to receive interest on loans (usury), to own other people as property, or to work out who is and who is not allowed to have sex with whom.

Remember too just how few human beings it is. You may have heard the old joke about Moses tottering exhausted down Mount Sinai and saying to the assembled people 'The good news is that I've got him down to ten; the bad news is that adultery is non-negotiable'. The point worth noticing here is that this is *a very twentieth-century story*: from all the historical understanding we have, it is clear that to the Hebrews the non-negotiability of clause 7 was not interesting – they were infinitely more concerned with negotiating clauses 1 and 2 (only one God and no graven images). The sorts of moral questions we seem obsessed with are rather less than a flicker in the dynamic of the cosmos. Though this does not for one moment make them trivial or unimportant; it just puts them in perspective.

There is one more thing that makes drawing reasonable moral conclusions from the given-ness, from the revelation, of the creation difficult and delicate. As I mentioned in my Introduction, we have abused, or rather restricted, the idea of reason itself. The feminist movement has throughout the twenty years of its present phase, battled strongly against the idea that 'logic' and particularly the rules of logic should be allowed the dominance that they have been. This has infuriated a great many people, but it is not really that we want to argue incoherently or stupidly; our resistance comes out of a very strong sense that the manipulation of this style of 'reasonableness' by those who are good at it frequently outmanoeuvres justice, truth and often common sense as well. This has been more than the childish sulk of those who cannot win and so want the rules changed; it has been a deep sense, and one I think that Christians also experience, that reason as it is understood in this context, does not always get you there. Certain things are simply not amenable to its methods.

Interestingly, during the same period of history in which we have been duped by a slightly bogus scientism into limited and restricted ideas of God, the same thing has been done to ideas of reason itself. We seem to have reached a point where the very word 'reason' has lost its holy resonance, and has been set up in opposition to ideas of beauty or spirituality. The seventeenth-century Carolingian divines, reasonable men if ever such there have been, did not treat reason so. I quoted Jeremy Taylor on this subject at the beginning of the book. In this context, Dr Whichcote's enchanting idea that 'reason is the candle of the Lord'[2] seems to convey something vital: reason is beautiful, a tool not a tyrant; it is meant to illuminate – to cast light; it belongs to God because 'God is light and in him there is no darkness at all'. Reason here is part of, rather than outside of, the cosmic drama. The self-contained formalisms of mathematical logic are not what Whichcote understands as 'reason'. Reason should not be seen as self-generating but as constructed and constructive; created and creative. It seems to me that 'when in awestruck wonder' we behold 'the worlds which God has made' and try to draw reasonable conclusions from them we do well to remember this.

Logical deduction, like the other sciences, has to be used appropriately. There is a simple analogy with Newtonian physics – it works perfectly, so long as you use it at the right scale and for the right ends; it doesn't necessarily work *everywhere* and *always*, and at all scales.

Too often, in an attempt to make things simpler for ourselves we have a tendency to be reductionist; to try and open things up and break them down into their smallest possible parts and then learn what can be learned about those parts. The danger is always that the whole may be – and often is – more than the sum of the parts; and worse still, you may have to destroy the whole in order to examine the parts. Reductionism has not, in the end, proved a very useful instrument in artistic or psychoanalytic disciplines. There seems little ground to suppose that the technique will prove useful in ethical theology, where the context gives meaning to the act.[3]

So for these and many other reasons I am extremely hesitant about sitting here and typing out a little algebraic formula such as: If God is X, then Y ethical position follows. Moreover there is a further danger in fragmentation: it is important that we do not end up contrasting, say, the God of mercy with the God of justice; or the God of order with the God of chaos; or – in this case – the God of creation with the God of law. Once again it seems to me that the constructions of post-Einsteinian physics are useful here – so much so that I am going to repeat a quotation I used earlier describing Bohr's theory of Complementarity which says that, sorry and everything to poor old mathematical logic, but indeed X can equal not-X.

> Quantum theory does not state that something – like light for instance – can be wave-like and particle-like *at the same time*. According to Bohr's Complementarity, light reveals either a particle-like aspect or a wave-like aspect depending on the context (i.e. the experiment). It is not possible to observe both the wave-like aspect and the particle-like aspect in the same situation. *However, both these mutually exclusive aspects are needed to understand 'light'.* In this sense light is both particle-like and wave-like.[4]

Luckily, we can understand the meaning of something without understanding all its parts. At the beginning of the 1939–45 war my father was part of a team put together to discover ways of making field radios more useable. Until the outbreak of hostilities it had been assumed that radio operation required highly technical skills because it was thought that you had to understand the theory in order to work the machinery. The team did itself out of a job rather quickly by leaving out all the engineering, electronic and radio-wave theory and just creating a list of instructions. This worked perfectly satisfactorily; and is a rather nice example of how human beings do not need to know everything in order to do something. For instance, you can drive a car without being a mechanic capable of explaining the working of the clutch, or tune in your TV without an advanced diploma in electronics. In a short book like this (or even a very long one, unlike this) it is impossible to talk about everything, and the triune nature of God makes drawing conclusions from one particular aspect or activity of God tricky. In the end salvation comes from the grace of God in the events, in the story of, the Incarnation and it is probably to that story and to the nearly 2,000 years of meditation on it, rather than to the wider reaches of space and time, that we should look for ethics.

So I am not going to attempt to read off an ethical code from the material I have outlined. Instead I want to talk about responses; about how we might *respond* to, react to, the Big-Enough God in her particular revelation through creation.

An immediate and necessary response is a humbled and shaken ejaculation of 'Oh wow'. The same sort of 'wow' that I suggested would be a poet's response to the creation narrative. This wowed posture, it seems to me, is what is meant by that odd word 'joy'. For people who have difficulty in assuming this posture I can recommend the exercise of drawing up a list of things for which it would be insane to give thanks, but which are obviously extraordinary. I will give you three of my favourites to start you off:

(1)   Once upon a time someone invented mayonnaise.

It may not have struck you what an extraordinary thing this is, but think about it. While you do, be sure to bear in mind that in rural societies every egg is precious, and every drop of olive oil has been pressed out by the feet of children who doubtless complained ceaselessly as they stamped.

Nonetheless, and for no apparent reason, it occurred to someone in Mahon on Minorca, without an electric blender, that if you wasted a great number of egg yolks by pouring olive oil on to them very slowly while half breaking your wrist with a whisk, the resulting mixture, far from being yellowish and perfectly revolting, would be white and fluffy and taste delicious with cold meat, hard-boiled eggs and particularly cold poached salmon.

Legend tells that mayonnaise was first made for a passing king, but this seems to me improbable. It is most unusual for any cook to start messing about with unlikely experiments when a king is waiting for his dinner; and your rivals – jealous that you got the job – are more than half hoping your soufflé will flop, and a small but perfectly formed slug will sneak into the salad and lurk under a rose-cut radish.

But then what circumstances are probable? Mayonnaise is not something you could discover through neglect, like Stilton cheese; nor through poverty, like bacon; nor through impatience, like new potatoes. Nor is it something that anyone can possibly have imagined first and then pursued determinedly through experiment. It is the unlikely consequence of careful persistence in an apparently pointless exercise. It is the joyful result of a creative application of hope, faith and love.

If I get to heaven I shall seek out this passionate soul, searching among the angels for one whose wings have that particular soft and lustrous sheen, and thank her. For it gives me some vague notion of how God must have made the world – smashing whole galaxies, more precious than eggs; slowly pouring in the dust of trampled stars and patiently stirring the primaeval goo – simply for delight and to see how it turned out.

(2) There are 9 planets and 47 moons in our solar system. (Actually there are more: the Voyager spacecraft photographed several extra moons around Saturn, but their orbits are not known and they are not named yet.) They *all* spin in the same direction except one: Triton, Neptune's giant moon, orbits its planet in reverse; which means that it is rotating the other way from Neptune itself. All that distance away, across cold space and out into the dark where the sun's light is as frail as moonshine, Triton—wrapped in crimson oceans of liquid nitrogen, down which sail majestic great blue-white icebergs of frozen methane—spins alone in a different direction.

(3)   God so loved the world that the Word (which was in the beginning and was with God and was God) became flesh and dwelt among us, full of grace and truth, and we beheld that glory, glory as of the only Son from the Father.

All these things are more or less pointlessly amazing. The only proper response is not 'thank you', but 'Oh wow'. They are not reasonable, or kindly; they are ridiculous, incongruent, magic. They make me not grateful, but joyful. Perhaps we should all go around not counting blessings only but counting the number of things that make us go 'Oh wow' in the course of each day.

The word 'joy' is derived from an Old French and Middle English word meaning 'jewel'. Joy is the treasure buried in the field, the pearl of great price. In the parable, once the merchant knows about the jewel he simply sells all he has to purchase it. This is not one of the parables about the cost of discipleship; it is quite the reverse. Once you have identified the treasure getting hold of it is entirely obvious, is no more than a sound investment. The problem is only in finding a good metal detector.

The traditional metal detector offered by the experts is gratitude, thanksgiving. When I was first taught to pray I was instructed always to begin with praise and thanksgiving, and I'm sure that this is right. As a teenager I was obliged to learn large chunks of the Book of Common Prayer by heart and I remain grateful for that. Its finest passages are often those of gratitude, and the General Thanksgiving remains a touchstone for me despite, or even because of, the difficulties I have with its language. It works especially well on days when I don't actually feel grateful for anything much; it has a sense of proportion and scale that is joyful in itself.

> Almighty God, Father of all mercies, we thine unworthy
> servants do give thee most humble and hearty thanks for
> all thy goodness and loving kindness to us and to all
> men. We bless thee for our creation, preservation and all
> the blessings of this life; but above all for thine
> inestimable love in the redemption of the world by our
> Lord Jesus Christ, for the means of grace and for the

hope of glory. And we beseech thee give us that due
sense of all thy mercies that our hearts may be
unfeignedly thankful and that we shew forth thy praise
not only on our lips but in our lives by giving up
ourselves to thy service and walking before thee in
holiness and righteousness all our days.[5]

However, despite the obvious truth of all this, the trouble with
gratitude is that, as we all know, it does not make a very good
basis for a relationship. When I was a child we were expected
each Boxing Day to sit down and write thank you letters for all
our Christmas presents (as I still expect my own children to
do, I should add). As we had a very large selection of aunts,
uncles, godparents, etc. it was a lengthy process and by the
end of it I often wished they hadn't given us presents at all –
especially as I often felt that it was more effort for me to write
than it had been for them to get hold of the present and post
it. I'm not sure that my relationship with this extended family
was not soured from the outset by this demand for gratitude.

The most poisoned form of this obligatory gratitude is
parents who expect their children to be grateful for 'everything I have done for you'. How many teenagers have fled
from rooms shrieking that they had never asked to be born in
the first place? How many of us adults transfer some of those
feelings to God? – a sort of subterranean resentment at the
endless obligation to be grateful for something we never really
wanted in the first place: our creation, our preservation, and
especially our redemption. Too much of Christianity stresses
Jesus' suffering for our sins so we ought to be jolly grateful. I
think there is not enough stress on Jesus' delight in us, on that
natural desire to do something extra special for the beloved
other which is the hallmark of being in love, not to earn their
gratitude but to please them, to make them joyful. Oddly
enough we are endlessly instructed not to do good deeds for

the sake of thanks but for the love of righteousness alone. Why should not God do the same?

Actually, if you ever feel these sorts of resentments it is worth telling God about them, out loud if possible – though try and find a fairly discreet place as you may get some funny looks. Apart from the honesty involved you will be amazed how quickly you start sounding like your adolescent self and this will make you laugh and restore some sense of proportion. It will also reveal how limited we are by using such exclusively parental language about God; how much our spirituality is formed by our perceptions of our parents and our least favourite schoolteachers. In that tiny space of rueful self-knowledge a little joy might just get a chance to sneak in.

Of course gratitude, thanksgiving, is important, but it is not enough. It is not big enough. This year, partly because I have wanted to seek comfort and companionship from someone else who has made the awkward journey from Anglicanism to Roman Catholicism, I have been reading about John Henry Newman. I have learned a great number of interesting and good things about that extraordinary courageous soul. Since his death there have been various moves within sections of the Roman Catholic Church to advance his canonization, but so far they have not been very successful. One of the reasons offered for this failure is that he wrote so much that no one can face working through it all to see if he said anything faintly heretical: we must hope this is not true. Another, more interesting, explanation of the failure is that Newman, despite his many sterling qualities, failed to manifest the joy which is considered a necessary mark of true saintliness. Newman is by no means alone in this failing.

Yet, interestingly, and – in the light of the way in which Jesus' motivations are usually presented to us now: 'He died that we might be forgiven, he died to make us good, he died that we might go to heaven' and so on and so forth – oddly, one of the few truly functionalist explanations that Jesus offered for his Incarnation and forthcoming death was: 'These things I have spoken to you that my *joy* may be in you and that *your joy may be full.*'

The fruits of the Holy Spirit, Paul tells us, are

> love,
> joy,
> peace,
> patience,
> kindness,
> goodness,
> faithfulness,
> gentleness,
> self-control.

Circle the odd one out.

For me at least, joy is the odd one out here, for several reasons. One of them is that it is the only item on the list that I do not think of as a virtue: a virtue being something that we recognize as requiring strength and application – both ours and God's – to have and to develop. Joy alone I tend to treat as something that comes and goes entirely from outside. I feel it or I do not feel it. I feel good when I do and sad when I do not, but it all comes randomly as gift, in a different way from the others. This may suggest that I have a somewhat Pelagian attitude to virtue. I am afraid that may be true: a solid Presbyterian childhood does not go away; you end up with a real love of Scripture and an overdose of the Protestant work ethic. Even so there remains a delicate language problem. All grace, and all graces, come as free gifts, and yet we have to co-operate in their incorporation. Both sunny weather and physical fitness are free gifts, but one requires only appreciation and the other the effort of going to the gym. I am trying to imply that while patience and self-control, for example, fall into the gym category; we act as though joy, like the weather,

161

falls on the just and unjust alike. In this context, joy, like the rain, often seems unfairly distributed:

> The rain it raineth on the just
> And also on the unjust fella;
> But chiefly on the just because
> The unjust steals the just's umbrella.[6]

I do pray, or try to pray, for an increase in all the other fruits of the Spirit, but I have to admit that I seldom pray for joy. I pray not to be unhappy; I pray that the things that make me unhappy will go away; but it is an absence of unhappiness, rather than an overflowing abundance of pure joy that I pray for; a negative not a positive thing.

Joy is the odd one out for another reason. It is the only grace on Paul's list that has no obvious opposite: hatred, enmity, impatience, cruelty, wickedness, betrayal, violence and self-indulgence. But joy? Misery is not really the opposite. Unhappiness is not, like the others, a sin; it is inevitable, a built-in fact of being human. By joy I do not mean happiness. Sad and bad things happen to me as to you, to which the only proper correct response is truly grief and misery, and this should not be denied. 'People who talk at grief, instead of holding hands with grief are a menace. Words come later, but only after tears.'[7] Happiness, like grief, is part of the process: a weather gift, not a gym gift. Neither Paul nor the gospel writers refer much to happiness and unhappiness in this sense, but they do refer to an obligation to be joyful. By joy I mean, I want to mean, something about the area called 'hope, faith and love' – a product, as it were, of the struggle to engage with and live with these harsh and demanding virtues.

Joy is a theological virtue because it is so much of God, so purely of God that the Devil is hard put to think of anything even remotely attractive to replace it with. Armed with joy we may truly laugh at the Devil, and that itself will increase our joy.

I should say here, perhaps, that I believe in the Devil – not the horns and tail bit necessarily, which seem to me to be in exactly the same category as God's beard and white hair, but I do believe. This is an extremely unfashionable thing to believe in, actually. Once at a conference of feminist theologians we were invited to describe what we saw as important feminist theological projects that we would like to see ourselves engaging with. (The answers were extremely interesting and varied: in particular, questions about how forgiveness was meant to work in the face of unrepentance; and issues about the difference between power and authority – these are still subjects that require our earnest attention.) I said I wanted to see some work done on inclusive language about the Devil – de-sexing Satan so to speak. There was something of a silence. Yet it seems to me that if we really want to create a language of equality, of inclusivity, then we must bring our attention to bear closely on sin and how it functions; claim it, so to speak, since if we cannot address sinfulness as such then we cannot address virtue either. It does not make much sense to me to talk about affirming my goodness, if I have projected all my badness on to something else – the institution, or capitalism, or sexism for example. I do believe in the Devil and one of the things I believe about her, for reasons that will be clear by now, is that she has an extremely limited imagination. So the infernal failure to think of a sin to throw into the balance against joy, which has so much to do with imagination and laughter and creativity, is not really surprising.

What I want to argue is that joy is in fact an ethical imperative in response to God's creative power as revealed in the whole created universe. It is an imperative, and it is a virtue – not only the right response, but also the proper response. Because it is a virtue enjoined on us by revelation, we have some sort of obligation to develop it and show it forth.

However, before I talk about joy any further there is something I feel it is proper to tell you about myself. There is always a danger with people who have an inclination towards being hysterical or agitated depressives (using that word at least semi-technically) that they overload their moments of exaltation with inflated meaning: that what they choose to call mysticism, or some other grand name like joy, is in fact no more than over-excitement. This should not encourage us to be sceptical about all mystical experiences, but to recognize they may sometimes emanate from states of mind which another person may simply be grateful not to have to endure. Recognizing in myself certain such tendencies I want to clarify that (1) I do not think it is that sort of joy I am trying to talk about and (2) I may very well be deluded.

It is of the nature of joy, born out of contingency and risk and uncertainty, that it is very difficult to pin a solid meaning onto it, let alone stabilize it long enough to take a hard look at it. This is a bit like the butterflies stuck neatly through with pins in glass display cases – it is true that one may thus admire the beauty of the butterfly's wings, but to do so the very butterfly-ness of the butterfly is destroyed. Another parallel would take us back to Heisenberg's Uncertainty Principle, which I discussed in Chapter 1: at the subatomic scale you cannot tell *both* where something is and how fast it is going somewhere else. There are close analogies between this and the dancing of joy. Joy, it seems to me, is tricky, and I mean that word very precisely – elusive, allusive, mind-boggling, sleight-of-hand stuff. This is partly because joy is extremely hard to abstract from its context and the emotion of feeling it. While all virtues require embodiment, incarnation, impersonation, to be understood fully, to be fleshed out, it is nonetheless more or less possible to imagine and describe abstractly what we mean by justice, or courtesy. Joy is much harder.

Feminist writers have a great attachment to the game of

etymology: to exploring the original meanings of words and noticing how they have been corrupted; or by devising new meanings and new uses of words.[8] It is rather a good game and can be a lot of fun, especially when it is played with real wit. But by and large I don't, in the end, find it very useful. Or rather it is useful, but the price you have to pay is too high. I can argue till I am blue in the face that the word 'gossip', for example, means something very positive. Indeed it originally meant the woman who accompanies another woman in labour, who talks with her throughout the long task, and whose particular job it is to receive and make welcome the newborn child if the medical attendants are busy with the mother. Since this might often mean carrying the newborn infant with all possible speed to the priest for baptism, the derivation becomes more sensible (gossip equals God + sib: a God-relative, a godmother). This history is very nice to know, and a good example of how dominant power structures, in this case sexist ones, tend to derogate the experience of oppressed groups. No one who has been in labour will think for one moment that there is much connection between the people who support you there, talk you through that place, and 'light or trivial chatter generally of a dishonest or un-kindly sort'. Nonetheless language, like so many other things, is not a static abstracted purity, but a living and therefore growing part of culture, and we cannot wrest this word or any other away from their lived use and just start using them to mean what we might want them to mean— i.e., a wonderful and rich women's tradition—regardless of that development.

This is important at the moment because of the post-structuralist insistence on the entirely arbitrary nature of language – that there is no real link between a thing and its name. I am fairly certain that, as with many of the other phenomena I have discussed, there is indeed a link – it is not arbitrary, but nor is it pre-given. It is forged in the use, it constructs meaning and personality and is constructed in its turn, and it is vital to the whole search for meaningfulness that we hold on to this historical shaping without which the words will indeed fail, and all the songs with them.

Although I have this suspicion that etymological juggling does not get any of us very far, I'm going to tell you something about the etymology of the word joy which you can perhaps try to read not as scientific linguistics but as poetry. The word joy is cognate not only with the word 'jewel' as I have already commented, but also with the modern French word *jouer*, 'to play'.

Joy is not just the treasure buried in the field, the pearl of great price. Joy is the game, the playing, between God and God's creation; it is the movement of delight and imagination and learning and power, like any game.

Alla Bozarth-Campbell, whose work I have mentioned before, tells a rather helpful story about her childhood which she feels may explain her very direct and vivid spiritual experience. She was brought up in a family with a strongly Marian devotion. As a tiny child she misheard the words of the *Ave Maria*: instead of 'Holy Mary Mother of God, pray for us sinners now and at the hour of our death' she thought the invocation ended 'Holy Mary Mother of God, play with us sinners now and at the hour of our death'. A very different and, for so young a woman, a very much more delightful prayer. This interconnectedness of preciousness and playfulness seems to me to reach to the centre of what I am wanting to feel, that it is both my 'duty and my joy' to feel, as I contemplate the God who created this specific universe, and me within it, and part of it.

Joy is a jewel and a game.

I have already suggested that one way of understanding joy is to see it as the product, if that is the right word, of the struggle to engage with the great virtues of hope, faith and love, in the light of the chancy risky universe in which we appear to be living. I would now like to explore this a little further.

If I have correctly understood the contingent nature of so much of our knowledge, the ground of our *hope* can no longer rest on some promise given in the past, of future security as a reward for good behaviour in the present. Hope lies rather in accepting that God's engagement in the creation gives us not just the right, but the obligation to create and sustain the future. Although he would not have used this sort of vocabulary I think this is perhaps what Augustine was after in that extraordinary and beautiful phrase 'Hope has two lovely daughters – courage and anger'. This is Augustine, remember, who accepts God's foreknowledge almost to the point of affirming predestination in the Calvinistic sense. Augustine sees salvation as being so entirely a mark of God's generosity that he can argue with terrible if painful sincerity that saying it is unfair that the unbaptized babies should go to hell is to question both the justice and the mercy of God; instead we should pause in abject gratitude and give thanks that *anyone at all* gets to go to heaven. Yet this same Augustine says that hope has two lovely daughters, courage and anger. Hope is the basis for taking responsibility; for claiming our capacity to create, to make a genuinely new thing. It is also the springboard for trying to act justly; and for accepting absolutely our incorporation into each other. It is not simply that we share with each other a common humanity, but that individually we have *no* humanity without each other.

Is it too much to require of ourselves that we hope constantly without knowing what it is that we hope for? One difficulty is that we do not have the least idea of the timescale, and anthropocentricity has compounded the problem. If the real purpose behind the creation of the universe was to produce humanity and train it up until fit for something better, it is hard to place much positive hope in so tortuous and bizarre a God. Billions and millions of years, the deaths of galaxies, the slow crawl out of the primaeval ooze just for the blink in passing of solitary souls on a journey to elsewhere? If, on the other hand, we can abandon so mechanistic and functionalist a viewpoint, take a different sense of the timescale and infuse that whole process with God's delight and joy, it all looks very different. It becomes much more like an adventure.

We have lost a true sense of adventure. In some ways this was an inevitable consequence of exploring and mapping the whole world; there seems to be no place for the adventurer to go. Space travel, though exciting, is not adventurous in the old sense: apart from being too expensive, the astronaut is too passive, not free to make sudden, wild decisions. Now the adventures have to be more internal, but do not be afraid – it is worth keeping in mind that at the very moment that a physical New World was being explored, discovered, in the lands of sunset, Ignatius of Loyola, Teresa of Avila, John of the Cross and many other Spanish spiritual adventurers were opening up new lands in the interior world: places full of battles and castles and darkness and danger. Originally an adventure meant something that happened to one outside one's control, by happenstance, by chance or fluke. The heroes of classic adventure stories are courageous, out-rageous, laconic, restless and free-spirited. Most of all they seem to want to know what will happen next. What does happen next is usually horrendous – dragons, deserts, loneli-ness, monsters, poverty, humiliations, crucifixions – but this does not seem to deter them in any way. On the contrary, they seem to take their motto from the Psalms:

> Blessed are those who going through the vale of misery,
> use it for a well; and the pools are filled with water.
> They will go from strength to strength and unto the God
> of Gods appeareth everyone of them in Zion.[9]

They are frequently stunned by ill fortune, the malice of the opposition, or by their own foolhardiness, but as soon as they are conscious again they are up and looking for another adventure, joyfully. Gratitude and humility in the confrontation with the meek passion of Christ must not allow us to forget the equally ancient images of him as an adventurer, a bold hero.

On the whole, in this genre of story it is not the safe homecoming that makes the adventurer joyful. Although the hero often does ride home on the last page, or sail into the harbour with the setting sun on the sails of the ship, this is not usually the point of the stories. On the contrary, as we see very clearly in the biblical adventures of Hagar, Abraham and Sarah's slave girl, it is precisely when she is driven out into the desert on a great unchosen adventure that the moment of joy strikes. It is there, at the very moment of greatest worry and desperation, that the joy crashes in and she becomes the *only* character in the whole of the Bible who 'sees God and lives'. She tastes the fullness of joy, and builds an altar in the windswept wastes of the desert, where it will never be seen and where there is nothing to sacrifice, just to celebrate that moment of joyful vision.

In the last ten years feminist critics have pointed out that there are serious moral problems, especially for women, with the ethos of the noble hero. Bits of these stories about lonely heroes, usually male, who travel out into the big bad world and 'defeat' the forces of darkness and receive upper-class virgins as their natural reward, are not really stories about risk and solidarity. They are self-rewarding tales which give a certain bogus glamour to wholesale destruction of whatever the hero's culture sees as uncivilized (dragons, Gorgons, Amazons, monsters – and in the more modern versions 'primitive people', 'natives' and wildlife) and their moral message runs directly contrary to what I have been trying to say. Yet even at their worst there is a hopefulness, a willingness to be like the Sons of Thunder, James and John, leaving their poor father in the boat and turning to the dangerous pathways without a backward glance, just because their names were called; or to be like Abraham and leave Ur of the Chaldees and go out into the desert places in hope, without knowing what will happen. We need to recapture that sense of adventure and hold tight to its truth. For anyone who loves their life will lose it, but anyone who is willing to throw it away will gain and keep it. Nothing will come of nothing. You have to go out and risk it all.

People used to know this. The Spanish conquistadors knew it. They went out in those tiny ships; they were blown away, stove in, starved, driven mad by thirst, taunted by monsters, broken by mountains, stabbed by their friends. Those things were real; but, distant as dawn dreams, there was the fabulous Kingdom of Eldorado: the land where the boy prince covered his beautiful body only with a coating of gold dust and washed each evening in a pool of clear water. That was worth the risk. And some of them, a few of them, came home with all the treasures of a New World; gold and emeralds and silver, sightings of the white unicorn, and visions of Amazons – the women who fought like men and worshipped the Great Mother.

Now it's not like that at all. If I wanted to discover a New World, They would make me take a two-way radio and wear a safety belt:

'Ring home every Friday', They'll instruct you, 'and if you don't we'll send a rescue party.'

'Safety first', They say, and 'Don't be foolhardy'.

'Wherever you go, we'll be there looking after you. *Whether you want it or not.*'

A theology and spirituality based on this mind-set is a hopeless, and therefore a joyless, one.

I've been reading recently about butterflies, which has taught me about the extraordinarily courageous adventure of the caterpillar. Like lots of kids I 'did' caterpillars in primary school. We fed the poor things until they were bloated, then we watched them build themselves their cocoons; and were encouraged to draw cute pictures of the sweet little caterpillar in there busily at work growing wings and lengthening its little stubs into antennae, ready to pop out.

This was a damn lie. Truly horrendous events occur inside a cocoon. First there is a total disintegration. Everything that was the caterpillar breaks down into chaotic matter, into a primal ooze, an amorphous smear. Only once the caterpillar has consented to that annihilation can the butterfly be constructed. The caterpillar has to risk all, for the emergence of its own beauty. That is why the butterfly used to be a symbol of the resurrection: you have to die, you have to be destroyed first, even if you're God.

Now a cocoon is supposed to be a place of safety and comfort, but then so is God. I don't get it. In the final count, it seems to me, God is the only danger big enough. If thine eye offend thee pluck it out. If thine right hand offend thee cut it off. Bend and break the will, discipline and scourge the flesh, face blindly the unknown, the enormous, the terrifying. Love your life and you'll lose it. Risk it and half-blind, mangled, limbless, maimed and maybe you'll just totter into heaven: the place of both annihilation and total knowledge. The risk is absolute, you'll get nothing else out of it – not pleasure, not health, not affection, not comfort – just beauty.

That it seems is our hope; that terrible beauty. Of course we do not like it: why should we? We are slightly brighter than the average caterpillar and have to act with consciousness because that is how it is to be human. It is an enormously scary hope, to have to live there at that balancing point, where to go even a little further will be too far, will be to crash into chaos and madness; where joy and beauty and pain get too tightly entangled and skid into masochism and derangement. This is a high price to pay, but it is still the jewel worth selling all that one has to obtain.

There is, nonetheless, some comfort to be found. I ended the last chapter with my dream about being a tightrope walker, and how tightrope walkers are taught that if you are frightened of falling, you fall; if you don't believe you will fall, you fall; and in the end whatever you do you will probably fall anyway. However, when I was learning about tightrope walking I also learned another tightrope walkers' slogan, which is: Anyone who performs without a safety net is either a show-off or an idiot.

Faith here can be seen as the safety net. Faith is an attempt, a frail and delicate attempt, to put form onto our hope; to accept that we cannot dance into the future, into the risk, alone and autonomous, because to do so is to reduce our personhood by cutting it off from its history. We are formed by that history, and we ought to want to enter into it because it is part of us. Freedom consists of voices that have been broken and blood that has been shed; freedom tastes of pain.

God cannot be spoken of, cannot be reduced to or claimed by our definitions, and still we try to speak what we feel that we think we know. Still in the enormous silence of the desert we sing like birds. And all our words are handed down to us through history, shaped by the tradition which Christians believe is a source of revelation. We do not have to re-create the whole language for God afresh in each little lifetime: it is there and we can enter into it, use it, lean on it, because we know it is true. The writer of the Gospel according to Matthew has an enormous faith of this kind. Jesus of Nazareth is the Messiah – and the gospel writer knows it, because Jesus fits into the description laid down in the tradition. The words that were spoken by the prophets are an assurance of reliability even though Jesus represents an entirely new act on the part of God. Such a faith releases us from dependence on our own 'personal experience', it gives shape and reassurance to our yearning, and it enables us to creep forward another inch or two. It protects us from insanity and the 'cliffs of fall' by giving us something to test our own beliefs against; faith gives us a bedrock of community which transcends our own particularities. At the beginning of this book I stressed that the revelation of God might not be coherent or logical but that it could not be contradictory. The deposit of faith gives us a working body of material against which we can test our own (and others') claims of orthodoxy.

This attitude I think is what Rosemary Ruether and Eleanor McLaughlin describe as 'radical obedience', in the ground-breaking introduction to their book *Women of Spirit*.[10] They are asking how we might live out an answer to the question, not about whether obedience is a virtue, but to whom that virtue is due: obedience to whom? Their complaint was not that women were not free to speak, but that women's voices had been silenced and the tradition was truncated, that faith had been made too small by the omission of a whole cloud of witnesses. Ursula Le Guin expresses this viewpoint rather more succinctly than I am managing to do:

> It is time you remembered that although I am a servant, I am not your servant.[11]

I can speak the words I speak – however critical, however impertinent – only because I have been given them in a long tradition, which I believe starts with the revelation that to know God is both an unachievable and a proper aspiration. Our faith is bonded into history, into time and space, and therefore is a part of our making. Feminists, both believing and unbelieving, are convinced that it is important to turn our attention to religion, and particularly (for those of us who are European) to Christianity, precisely because this belief, this faith, has created our language, our culture and therefore the persons that we are. Sheila Rowbotham, the eminent socialist feminist historian, expresses the need thus:

> There came the realization that we needed to resist not only the outer folds of power structures, but their inner coils. For their hold over our lives through symbol, myth and archetype would not dissolve automatically with the other bondages even in the fierce heat of revolution. There had to be an inner psychological and spiritual contest along with the confrontation and transformation of external powers.[12]

She would most certainly not want to call this 'faith', but I would. I have faith because it has been named, articulated, sustained through history by those whom I know to be my companions – that is fellow human beings who have laid down, however buried in dusty libraries, maps of the land that has to be travelled, so that however dangerous the road, however close to the edge of the chasm I walk, I do have a hint of a path, the possibility of a safety net which will help us all not to fall into the void of insanity or unspeakability.

Because there is faith, of that sort, because we are all joined into one, there is also the possibility of *love* and justice. Following Simone Weil, I am assuming here that justice can be described as the disciplined commitment to act towards all the people we do not know, have not met, and cannot ask for their opinion as though they were our lovers, as though we loved them in the more immediate and experiential sense of the word. Love now becomes more self-interested – in loving others I am loving myself, because I am created as person, as self, by the community of humanity past and present, and do not exist as person without that *koinonia*, that comradeship – and at the same time, more solid, more realist, materialist, than we usually dare to hope.

What I am arguing towards is a position that puts love, faith and hope – the moral virtues – firmly into the same basket as the whole of the creation. I sense a need to close the gap, heal the divide that we often try to maintain, for highly dubious motives, between the God of law and the God of love. In the beginning, the rôle of creator (lover) and the rôle of law-giver were inseparable, were united; both creativity *in action*, and law-giving *in justice* are the single action of God. That is why I suggested at the very beginning of this book that justice issues cannot be detached from metaphysical issues; that mysticism and ethics are closely bound together.

It seems to me that the engagement of keeping all these things in balance produces a strange mixture of humbleness and self-confidence; a willingness, a necessity even, to act even knowing that you cannot *know* whether your action is absolutely right, not because you have failed to inform your-self but because right is not absolutely absolute ever. Both Heisenberg's Uncertainty Principle and Cantor's Absolute Infinity can be applied to human conduct. This balance, this tightrope-walking act is productive of joy—we might even rashly call it holiness, but joy is easier and perhaps of more general application.

I therefore end with a few notes which develop the idea that there is an ethical directive, even imperative, to be joyful. Quite simply joy is a virtue and we must practise it, show it forth 'not only on our lips but in our lives'. Like any other virtue it is supernatural. We will not just receive it, but must make ourselves willing to receive; we must practise, develop our joy muscles in the moral gymnasium, rather than sit around hoping it will fall on the just and on the unjust alike.

Notes on the practise of joy

Firstly it is important to remember that there cannot be a DIY manual on joy. If joy is indeed a virtue it is thereby a grace, and we cannot do it, get it, on our own: it comes from God as gift. The only thing we can do at this level is pray. We can solicit the intercession of the saints, whom we believe to be full of the fullness of joy, and beg and beseech heaven to give us this grace, but we can neither earn it nor acquire it. However we can prepare ourselves to co-operate with God's generosity in the power of the Holy Spirit. This preparation, preparedness, is a rather odd thing. Alcoholics Anonymous have a faintly disturbing motto – 'Fake it and make it': act as though you already *felt* some particular emotion and the emotion will follow. The boundary between the lack of authenticity, insincerity, hypocrisy and an honest endeavour to act as we believe we ought even when we do not want to is a very narrow one, and it is particularly hard with joy to walk it in a soberly straight line. I am not talking about drumming up an emotion, but about training oneself to incorporate and act out a truth. Anyone interested in experimenting with any of the following suggestions, or others of their own, should bear this difficulty in mind.

(1) *Prayer* Simple old-fashioned intercessory prayer should not be underestimated. Ask God to make you joyful. Joy is a virtue that we need, and a gift we must be always ready to receive. One of the best ways of obtaining any gift is to make sure the giver knows that you want it. That mean old nursery proverb – 'I want never gets' – is not only untrue but leaves behind, even in people who think they have outgrown the nursery, a horrid legacy of inability to tell anyone you want something, and the more important the something is, the harder it feels to ask for it. Luckily for us, we are not in the nursery, God is not a nanny. In my experience God has impeccable manners, that out-of-date virtue of courtesy, and is unlikely to force upon us any gift we have not made clear that we want. The best way to get any virtue is almost certainly to pray for it. Pray continually, we are instructed, pray without ceasing. However it is important to remember that God has an extremely joyful sense of humour: to pray for joy with an

excess of solemn piety, with a total absence of self-irony and humour, is to ask for trouble.

(2) ***Happiness is normative*** This has to be the starting point. If we have any faith at all in the articulations of our tradition then that faith teaches us that God does indeed find us altogether wonderful and worth any amount of effort – even that of real suffering. This being the case we must accept that happiness is our natural, our normative, state. Truth is also normative; it is part of the nature of God in whose image we are being created. Therefore what we believe when we are happy is more likely to be true than what we believe when we are depressed. People are always talking about the ghastly doubts they endure when things go wrong in their lives. I do not think they should worry so much. Obviously if happiness is our truth and our goal then unhappiness is an abnormal condition and one in which we should not be too ready to trust our own judgements too much. We ruin times of possible joy, faith and love by remembering that when we were last miserable we did not find God so easy to believe in. Yet we seldom alleviate times of misery by reminding ourselves that when we were happy we found no particular problem with God. Thus Jesus' cry of desolation from the cross ought to be more encouraging and companionable than we usually find it: he would not have been fully human if he did not find pain, exhaustion and the approach of death somewhat undermining of a serene and confident faith. This realization ought, rationally, to apply not just to major disasters, like crucifixion and bereavement, but to little inconveniences as well. If we are bored, or cold, or sulky, or tired, or hungry we are less like the human beings God is in the process of co-creating with us than when we are interested, comfortable, playful and refreshed. We should bring to the former moods the convictions of the latter ones, in the faith, the simple knowledge, that this is when we are most like ourselves. This takes practise.

(3) ***Adoration*** I am so much not an expert on this (and I

do not mean this in the same way as I talked earlier about not being an expert, but an amateur, in physics or maths or sociology) that it seems more appropriate to direct the joy-seeker to other more distinguished practitioners. There are lots. Nonetheless adoration has to be a key concept here. By adoration I mean the disciplined, hard work of trying to pray some of the time in a way that looks only at God, and God's work, and that does so without self-seeking: without penitence, or gratitude, or request, or anything else – however good in itself, however appropriate and proper in its appropriate and proper place. It sometimes seems to me, however, that we have not been helped to assume this joyful stance by many of the great spiritual writers, who see such contemplation as the highest rung of a ladder up which we must be endlessly struggling. To live constantly in humble adoration probably does require such levels of discipline, but perhaps we should treat it more casually sometimes and begin by noticing that most of us are in this condition quite often. It is not that rare or exalted to take pleasure in something beautiful just because it is beautiful; or to laugh at something funny just because it is funny; or even to do both at once. In my limited experience God has a terrific sense of humour, a continual offering up of the richness and absurdity of being, and it is recognizing these moments and recognizing that they are gifts of the divine essence which seems to me the core of adoration. Adoration, at least at the start, is only making conscious something which is so ordinary to our nature that it tends to operate unconsciously.

It is also worth remembering that one of the things that it is to be human is to be different in one way or another from other humans. This means that there can be an infinite number of styles of approaches to adoration. Even within the traditional disciplines of spirituality there are a wide variety of angles to come at this: the *via negativa* of the writer of *The Cloud of Unknowing*; the passionate nuptial imagery of Teresa of Avila; the co-worker model of Ignatius of Loyola; the 'plaything of the child Jesus' – that superficially tiresome, deliberate 'littleness' of Thérèse of Lisieux. It seems paradoxical, but eminently satisfactory, that it is only through knowing oneself extremely well that one can find a way to self-forgetfulness.

(4) *Anti-individualism* When Margaret Thatcher as Prime Minister informed us that there was no such thing as society, there was only the individual and the family, she was – to put it bluntly – lying. Whether this was a deliberate and conscious lie or not I cannot be certain, but it is not true. It is not true quite simply because it is impossible. In the first place the family clearly is itself a 'society'; and in the second place because there is no way of becoming or being a human individual except through and within 'society': that is in association with other human beings. I have tried throughout this book to explain this connectedness. As a twentieth-century feminist it would clearly be improper (if not worse) to deny the many and real benefits of the Enlightenment, and Enlightenment concepts of human rights, but these benefits must not be allowed to overwhelm the dangers of rampant individualism. The language of personal fulfilment is curiously absent from the gospels; absent from there I suspect because the great strength of Judaism is the linking of the individual person to the history and destiny of the community. This highly pragmatic and unemotional certainty which so fundamentally informs the Hebrew Scripture, and thence the canon of Christian Scripture, is based on an understanding that 'we'll all go together when we go'. The most state-of-the-art contemporary science says the same thing. If we can move towards truly believing that, then all the pain of the universe will weigh more heavily upon us, heavily enough perhaps for us to take at least tentative steps towards establishing justice and peace in the world, which will –

though for us in the West at heavy expense – inevitably increase our joy.

Earlier I described one of Simone Weil's definitions of justice (acting towards the people we did not know, and so could not 'love', as though they were the people we did love). She also wrote of justice in a very different and rather unusual way: in any dispute there will inevitably be one 'side' with more power than the other; justice was what happened when the party with the most power acted – pretended – that this was not the case. This understanding of justice is very alien to the more usual understanding that justice is something that the oppressed have a 'right' to demand. Yet it offers some comfort to those of us white, Western, fed, educated people because it allows us afresh to participate actively in the pursuit of justice (instead of just sitting round, wallowing in guilt and waiting for some Marxist historical inevitability to do the work of justice to us and for us).

The understanding which the Hebrew people had, and which contemporary science reiterates, that we belong to each other, that we create and redeem each other not as acts of self-denial but as acts of affirmation of our true selves, is an important source of joy.

(5) *Have more fun* If the universe was indeed made rather more for delight and love than as a boys' public school or a painfully difficult assault course for tiny souls to toughen them up and get them fit for heaven, then 'having fun', far from being self-indulgent, becomes part of the proper response to what we have been given. It is meant to be fun. It will certainly be fun in heaven. We pray 'thy will be done on earth as it is in heaven' but we seem curiously reluctant to put this into any sort of practise. If we can develop and strengthen a conviction that we are, and are meant to be, co-creators of that heaven-on-earth, then having fun (even little fun – trying to eat doughnuts without licking our lips, for example, or trying to guess idiotic riddles – never mind big fun like good sex and

going to the theatre) becomes an entirely obvious exercise. Fun is not joy, but it is not happiness either: fun is something we can choose, as we cannot choose happiness, and it is a better form of joy training than the traditional gloomy self-denial and mortification enjoined on us by too many spiritual manuals. Indeed finding out what is fun – for me, for you, in the recognition of difference – is training not just in joy but in love itself: How can I delight my beloved? When my beloved wants to offer me something, what can I ask for? These are the questions that lie at the heart of loving; these are presumably the questions that God answers in creating the universe and all that is in it.

We cannot exactly say that there is a moral obligation to have fun, because it sounds too much like that awful moment when your mother puts on your mittens, pushes you out the door into the rain and says 'Now go and enjoy yourself'. Moral obligation and fun feel like polar opposites, but that is because we are fallen creatures, whose immediate inclination is too often not to enjoy ourselves, not to serve our own clear interests, not to do the thing we want to do. There is a symptom of depression called *anhedonia*: the inability to seek pleasure. It is the precise opposite of hedonism, and it is a recognized symptom of a serious illness.

I would like to see 'Today I failed to have fun, *x* number of times, alone or with others' inserted into every old-fashioned sin list that is still in print.

(6) *'Safety first'* may be a good motto for car driving, but it is fatal to holiness. Too often we use God as a sort of insurance policy, or a child's security blanket to keep away our night fears. The way the creation turns out to be, the Bible and the lives of the saints all conspire to teach us that there is no safety, and that when we seek it we are fooling ourselves. There is no safety but there is, in risk, a risky joy. Children in playgrounds and at fun fairs like to be a little scared: those screams of fear and of joy are very close. It is the readiness to

run risks – both physical and emotional – with open-hearted excitement, and the willingness to be surprised by *whatever* happens next, that wins the glittering prize: the vision of the glory of God.

'Considering how dangerous everything is, nothing is really very frightening', wrote Gertrude Stein (not a woman much quoted in moral exhortatory literature). If we can accept that at the centre, at the important places, there is no safety, then we do not have to waste time bowing down to false gods, but will be free to go out and live courageously at the edge of our humanity; where we can 'see God and live'. Courage is itself a source of joy, and we can seek it from the wild, the untamed God, who runs such risks for me. We need courage so that we can dare to leave the land of slavery and walk boldly and joyfully through the dangerous waters and the barren deserts. Only there can we learn to sing and laugh; for wherever we let God lead us will be our promised land.

(7) *Sensible consolations*   When I was first trying to learn to pray I was constantly warned against 'feelings', against emotions. It was not, I was told, meant to make me feel good, or even bad for that matter; it was not about feelings, not about experience, but an exercise of the will, a harsh and unlovely thing. I think I know now what these people were trying to tell me – that one could not judge the effectiveness of one's struggle to convert one's heart by the intensity of feeling, but only by the fruits of grace. However, I am still not sure that it was quite such good advice as it was meant to be. 'Sensible consolations', like too much pious talk, is an extraordinarily outmoded term. To start with it uses 'sensible' with a meaning quite different from the contemporary one: sensible consolations does not mean 'reasonable comforts', it means enjoyable sensations. I cannot think of a single relationship, other than ours with God, that anyone would expect to be without enjoyment. The feelings of warmth, safety, challenge, laughter, beauty, playfulness are marks of friendship; they do

not dictate against loyalty, faithfulness and the hard slog of loving – quite the contrary, they strengthen and succour such disciplines. No one who has had charge of a tiny baby imagines that anyone gets up for the fifth time in three hours at four in the morning, when the light is barely grey and very cold, leaving the smashed fragments of dreams and the warmth of well-deserved rumpled sheets to tend to a screaming dampish bundle, with spontaneous floods of pure delight. Of course such loving is a harsh and unfeeling reality; but at the same time such people also know that when one is welcomed by that huge, toothless and enchanting grin, by the bizarrely pleasant feeling of breast milk letting down, and the warm rumpled dampness of a nursing child, it is all the more possible to get up again 40 minutes later. The sensible consolations of nursing a baby seem to me, at the very least, a well-designed evolutionary device to secure the continued caring attentions of a necessary adult; and at best they are a grace and joy. Why should God be meaner and more devious than a three-month-old human being? Why should physical delight be treated as a dangerous snare and delusion?

If it is true, and it must be, that beauty and truth are ultimately one because 'the beauty of God is the cause of being of all that is', it seems to me that the more sensible consolations we can find on our long and dangerous journey the luckier we are. The willingness to go travelling, to run risks for the sake of a risky delight, is not in conflict with a love, a passion for the beautiful. Life is not a nasty but necessary chore to be hurried through as quickly as possible, but an extraordinary panorama of delight. God made it and found it good, and despite the corruption and ruin that it has become, it is worthy of our attention and we are worthy of its beauty. We need all the sensible consolations we can get; and we would be both foolish and ungrateful not to seek them out and wallow in their comforts whenever we can. In particular, indulgence in the consolations of art – especially including Scripture and liturgy; of the magical and improbable diversity of matter that the contemporary sciences offer us; and of sex and friend-ship, is all conducive to joyfulness.

Friendship is perhaps the least acknowledged of these. The great Churches lift up art to the heavens, and proclaim the beauty of God: the sun and moon, the stars of heaven, the great waters of the oceans and the beauty and generosity of the land have from the beginning given shape to praise and glory. The intimate connection between the language of lovers and the language of heaven has been recognized in the great nuptial imagery of the mystics. Meanwhile friendship continues to be underestimated. This is why the recognition that we are fellow-workers, co-creators with God of the continually new and renewed structures of the cosmos, which the contemporary sciences re-emphasize for us, is so impor-tant. A strange thing has happened in the twentieth century: we are proud to have cast off the reticence and shame which made it impossible for our great-grandparents a hundred years ago to talk about sex, but we seldom notice that we have replaced this shame by a deep embarrassment about our souls. We seldom talk openly about 'how I pray'. This is a new secrecy; and we should notice at least how strange it is that it should feel easier to discuss what gives me orgasms than what gives me joy in God. Companionship on the journey, a place for religious intimacy, for sharing that part of ourselves, is a precious gift and we should seek it out for the consolation, edification and joy that it provides us with and, of course, we should seek it out simply because it is fun.

'Do you believe in angels?' a friend of mine said to me quite casually as we chatted of this and that over dinner recently and I found myself blushing. 'Is that a serious question?' I asked rather sharply – because I was ashamed, as though I had been caught out picking my nose. When I looked up at him, trying not to blush, I knew it was a real question and he really wanted to know. 'Yes' I said, almost coyly. 'So do I' he said, and we both laughed at the difficulty of all this. We laughed and there was a flutter of rose-scented feathers across the restaurant, a quick harp riff, and a smile of pure joy hovering in the air. I wish I could do it, so openly, like a child asking about sex on top of the No. 6 bus just as it swings round the Aldwych and every single passenger holds their breath waiting to hear how the poor adult will answer. My friend has a transparency of faith, a childlike fascination and curiosity in such sensible consolations which open up new fields of joy for me.

(8) *The second naïvety* For most of my theological lifetime the demythologizers have been at work: approximately 87.4 per cent of everything we have believed is to be branded 'mythology', immature, childish and lacking scientific bottom. Superstition. Irrelevance. The miracles, especially those in the gospels, are prime material for such treatment: it never seems to occur to the demythologizers that turning water into wine by the ordinary method (fermentation) is every bit as extraordinarily startling, bizarre, even 'miraculous', as what happened at the wedding feast in Cana. The demythologizers absolutely fail to recognize that a little more awe and wonder, a little more immaturity and magic, an honest delight in lucky (and of course virtuous) Daniel surviving the night while the lions prowl and roar and do not hurt him, would do none of us any harm.

I have a friend whose parents would not let their children hang up stockings for Father Christmas because 'it is a lie'. I consider such a childhood deprived. My son, now aged twelve, seems to me to have a more healthy attitude to this sort of thing: he does not believe in Father Christmas from 1 January through until 23 December – for the remaining week of the year he believes absolutely and fundamentally in Father Christmas. He says it is more fun that way. He is right.

Demythologizers have a rather arid understanding of what it is to be a human being and of what it is to tell the truth. The high-tech world and well-sanitized faith in which they apparently want us to live may be cleaner and safer than the scruffy old one, but it is not very joyful. I know I am being unfair, and I am not – however it may seem – really criticizing true biblical scholarship; yet I do believe that demythologizing has now gone far enough, has in fact gone too far. We are in urgent need of bit of re-mythologizing.

Scientism is a myth too, a myth as pernicious as any other sort of fundamentalism. Any stance towards the world which holds that it can be read off and lived at one level only, and that God must be forced to perform according to the requirements of that level, is dangerous to our wholeness. It is a denial that God is – of necessity, of divine ontology – beyond the boundaries of our categorizations. Biblical fundamentalists may be attacked for wishing to confine God's activities to those laid down in the Bible; but rationalist fundamentalists are attempting to do the same thing. They want to limit God to what we know how to articulate within the structures of a distinctly restrictive epistemological code. In fact our ability to think, to imagine, to create mythologically is becoming severely restricted, and this is worrying.

For example, our idea of what is now called a 'rôle model' is being reduced to wanting someone or something 'just like me'. The Virgin Mary is a victim of this process, I think. Her virginity is seen as an insult to our sexuality; her Assumption and Coronation as an added insult to the shame of our mortality. This is an entirely modern problem; myth does not work this way. In an extraordinary number of mythologies, for example, the guardian power of women in childbirth is a virgin. For the Greeks it was Artemis, on whom women in labour called. It was to that point of physicality, of fleshliness that they imaginatively required her to bring the power of her untouchedness, her almost brutal purity – Actaeon was hunted and killed by his own hounds just for the misfortune of seeing her naked. Such women understood how myth could work for them.

The early Church knew precisely what it was up to, though how consciously we cannot know, when it chose Ephesus as the place to name Mary as *theotokos*, the virgin god-bearer, the Mother of God. Ephesus was an ancient shrine of Artemis, also called Diana ('Great is Diana of the Ephesians' screamed the mob who thought Paul might take this powerful inter-cessor away from them). Actually though, in the Middle Ages it was not Mary who was the saint, the guardian of childbirth – it was Margaret of Antioch. She, it was believed, defended her virginity to the point of death, refusing to marry a patriarch, a king. As the executioner's axe was poised above her neck she was luckily snatched up and swallowed whole by a passing dragon. Her purity offended the dragon's digestive system and when it had flown away to a distant island it opened its mouth and set her free. Women turned to her with their laborious prayers because she had walked free and untouched through the narrow dark throat of the dragon, through its huge stretched red mouth and safely out into the sunshine. Far from killing the ferocious dark power, she made a garland of flowers, looped it round the dragon's neck and led him, docile as a lap-dog, back through the city. It is at our peril that we lose the capacity to understand what is going on here. We need to draw strength from such signs of difference, from such luminous and sustaining stories.

I had a debate once with some male clergy about the virginity of Mary, which they felt it was important to deny. At first they gave a functionalist reason for this – that it encouraged Docetism (the heresy that teaches that Jesus did not really become human but was a God in fancy dress). I said that this, while true, did not seem to be a current problem: I had not met any Docetists recently. I had, however, encoun-tered lots of Arians (the reverse heresy – Arius did not accept the co-eternal nature of the Logos, but believed that Jesus was 'created' rather than 'begotten', and so was not fully God). I reminded them of the old slogan – 'Those who are not Marian are Arian'. At this point in the debate they switched ground to what seemed to me a more honest, if less high-minded, position: they wanted Mary not to be a virgin so that Jesus could come into the world 'just like them', could be born in 'the usual way'. This seemed to me to open a whole new can of worms. I feel there is something deeply sexist about all this, since from the point of view of women, Jesus did indeed get born in entirely the usual way – down a woman's vagina and out between a woman's legs just like everyone else. The only difference being that maleness was made redundant in this myth. Was it this that they found intolerable? More to the point here, however, was this desire to identify entirely with Jesus, to take him over, make him over, reduce him to being 'just like them'.

What this is meant to say to women's incorporation in Christ is problematic: the old slogan 'that which is not assumed is not saved' is important – if Jesus has to be exactly like me, then anyone who is not exactly like me, because of gender, class, race or even personality, is less incorporated than I am. Still more worrying, though, is the complete inability here to understand a mythopoeic structure, to see that difference also means universality; that the virginity of Mary is not about biology, but about meaning, about symbol and metaphor; which is necessarily embedded in narrative, in story. Feminists are frequently accused of this, of trying to remake the stories so that they more closely 'match' with our experience. We do do it, more often than we should, although I would argue that having been excluded for 2,000 years from 'being like Jesus' we have some excuse. It is not so often noticed how much rationalist demytholozigers do it. The weighty presence of their personal agenda is not challenged often enough. Because they cannot make the lame walk, the blind see, the deaf hear; because they cannot set the captives free nor proclaim the acceptable year of the Lord, Jesus is not going to be allowed to do any of that stuff either. Because they cannot believe in angels, or in miracles, neither can anyone else. Poor lambs!

Seriously though, we urgently need to reclaim the art of telling stories, and hearing stories, about the divine if we are to have a joyful faith. Imagination, creativity, narrative seems to be the way God is in the world of matter. Or rather it seems to be the way the world of matter is and therefore how we are. An elderly friend of mine once sat through an intellectual session of demythologizing in slightly grumpy silence. At the end of it he turned to me troubled and said 'I don't understand their problem; they seem to want to believe in less and less. My problem is finding enough new things to believe in.'

The naïvety of childhood is the naïvety of ignorance; the second naïvety is to become innocent, knowing that while ignorance is an unfortunate fact of life, innocence is a demanding virtue: open-minded, simple-minded without loss of knowledge or integrity, becoming as a little child again without the security blanket of lack of data; with a determination to find the world beautiful, magical, wild beyond dreams, dancing its complex patterns of truth, weaving its multicoloured threads of discourse so that all things can be true and we can once more be ravished by the beauty of God as revealed by choice, by loving power, in the whole dense, disorderly, chaotic and joyful universe.

I really do believe in angels and I am glad that I do. They and other imaginative constructs of mind and heart are sources of joy, the joy that I am completely certain makes the shape and meaning of the creation.

> The angels keep their ancient places,
> Turn but a stone and start a wing;
> 'Tis ye, 'tis your estrangèd faces
> That miss the many-splendoured thing.[13]

We are estranged. Fear has estranged us from our world, which is God's world. We Christians have been warned off our own territory. We have been scared to the point that we do not dare to lift a stone and look at what is underneath. It is more likely, as a matter of fact, to be a woodlouse than any of the more traditional angels we have been taught not to believe in. But angels are primarily messengers from God – and, behold, even woodlice may prove angelic:

> *Hemilepistus reaumuri* [is] a woodlouse which inhabits the parched deserts of North Africa and Asia Minor. This is the driest habitat conquered by any species of crustacean and it is probably the exigencies of surviving in such a harsh environment – particularly the need to dig and then maintain possession of a burrow – which have predisposed the evolution of social behaviour in this highly successful animal. In so doing, *it provides one of the few examples of paternal care* among invertebrates.[14]

'I am come that you may have life, life more abundantly.' 'These things I have spoken to you that my *joy* may be in you and that your joy may be full.'

There is nothing to be afraid of in a world so intricately made that even the woodlice under the stones speak to us of the social and parental life of the God who created them. There is evolution, and indeterminacy, and generosity, and chance. There is risk and beauty and joy. Gambling on the God who has so gambled on us does not seem so risky in the end.

Notes

1. Christopher Marlowe, *The Tragical History of Doctor Faustus*, Act I, scene 1.
2. For a fuller discussion of the seventeenth century's understanding of reason see Basil Willey, *The Seventeenth-Century Background* (Chatto & Windus, 1934), especially chs 7 and 8.

3. For example, the *act* of heterosexual penetrative coitus is the same whether it is performed inside or outside of marriage, and with or without the consent of one or other party (always, as it happens, the woman). Morally however, it is perfectly possible to draw a clear distinction between rape and consensual sex; and Christianity has found no problem drawing a sharp distinction between identical acts performed before and after a specific ceremony called marriage. Reducing sexual acts to their constitutive biological contents is unhelpful, both to sexually happy couples and to rape victims.

4. Gary Zukov, *The Dancing Wu Li Masters* (William Morrow, 1979), p. 93.

5. The General Thanksgiving, Book of Common Prayer.

6. Lord Bowen: *Oxford Dictionary of Quotations*.

7. John Bowker, *The Meanings of Death* (Cambridge University Press, 1991), p. 42.

8. The US radical feminist Mary Daly is the mistress player of this game. In her books *GynEcology* and *Pure Lust* (both Beacon Press) she manipulates language exquisitely, wittily and usefully.

9. Psalm 84.6–7 (Book of Common Prayer).

10. Rosemary Ruether and Eleanor McLaughlin (eds), *Women of Spirit* (Simon & Schuster, 1979).

11. Ursula Le Guin, *Wizard of Earthsea* (Gollancz, 1971), p. 162.

12. Sheila Rowbotham, *Dreams and Dilemmas* (Virago, 1983), p. 189.

13. Francis Thompson, 'In No Strange Land'.

14. R. and K. Preston-Mafham, *The Encyclopaedia of Land Invertebrate Behaviour* (Blandford/Cassell, 1993), p. 161 (my emphases).

Sara Maitland is the author of a book on women and Christianity, *A Map of the New Country*, as well as fiction, including *Daughter of Jerusalem*, *Three Times Table*, *Ancestral Truths*, and *Angel Maker*.